PRAIS...

The Power of Natural Mentoring

"Our relationships shape who we become throughout our lives. This scientifically grounded, experientially rich book will help guide you as a 'natural mentor' for a younger woman or girl's life to effectively and enjoyably support their growth toward a life of meaning and resilience. Filled with illuminating and compelling examples, *The Power of Natural Mentoring* is a brilliant synthesis of a range of research fields that inform a practical toolkit of thriving to create relationships that will have a lasting impact and help not only the individual you mentor but also our world to become a more caring, compassionate place for all."
—**Daniel J. Siegel, MD**, *New York Times* best-selling author, *Mind, Aware, Brainstorm, The Developing Mind*, and *Mindsight*; co-author of *Parenting from the Inside Out, Whole Brain Child*, and *The Power of Showing Up*, Clinical Professor, UCLA School of Medicine, Executive Director, Mindsight Institute

"Christine Wagner's book is not just a primer on #NaturalMentoring for women and girls—it should be an international movement, especially now as more women are called on to lead. Supporting a young woman into her brilliance and helping her find her authentic voice has been the most important work of my life."
—**Mary Ellen Jones**, film and television producer

"I adore this book! Refreshingly practical, deeply inspiring, it's the exact manual every manager, coach, mother, sister, teacher, HR professional—every person who wants to make a difference!—has been waiting for. This book is going to change so many lives, including yours."
—**Jennifer Louden**, best-selling author of *The Woman's Comfort Book: A Self-Nurturing Guide for Restoring Balance in Your Life* and *Why Bother? Discover the Desire for What's Next*

"What a gift to girls and women everywhere. In *The Power of Natural Mentoring*, Christine Wagner has crafted an insightful and beautiful journey of empowerment and action for women and girls through storytelling, depth of experience, and intensive research. This book is an incredibly rich deep dive into self-discovery and reflection, as well as a practical guide to putting the tools into action. Most importantly, it gives girls permission to understand, love, and accept themselves for who they are."
—**Kelley Amadei**, founder, SparkShift: A Transformational Leadership Consultancy

"I have had the opportunity to see Christine Wagner's natural mentoring approach in action, and it is deep and important for girls and women. This book lays out the process in an easy-to-follow manner, and it is worth taking the time to use it. Girls need women's support, and this guide helps us be more effective."
—**LeAnne Grillo**, co-founder, Spaces for Change

The Power of Natural Mentoring should be rolled up in every young college woman's diploma or, even better, on the must-read list for every freshman college student. Christine Wagner has "nailed it" in terms of giving us a comprehensive understanding of what natural mentoring is and how it impacts young women, and a driving manual for how to make it happen efficiently and effectively. I so wish I had enjoyed the benefit and privilege of a natural mentor in my earlier life. This book gives us a thorough, clear understanding of what needs to become common practice in our culture today."
—**Julie Ashley**, MSW, RSW, Certified Brené Brown Facilitator, Ontario, Canada

"Christine Wagner's *The Power of Natural Mentoring* makes a compelling case for the necessity of trusted role models in the lives, development, and growth of successful female leadership in any realm. What differentiates this unique kind of "natural" mentoring is that these profound influencers are often already in young lives through organic, natural relationships. Sharing extensive interviews with women from all walks of life to demonstrate its effectiveness, this book offers a brilliant approach for the self-development journey: a five-step process called the "Thrive Cycle." While it can be walked side by side with a natural mentor and a girl or young woman as she gets her start in school, in her career, or through any life transition, the author particularly encourages women to first venture through the cycle alone to fully assess and further develop self-awareness from an adult perspective as part of preparing to assist the young person in her life."
—**Jenn Bajec**, founder, Thrive Theory Design

"What touched me most about *The Power of Natural Mentoring* was that I could see myself in both the young women being mentored and the natural mentors. The honest and vulnerable stories shared in the book showcase how connection with one other caring adult mentor can empower a girl to find her voice and progress on the journey of becoming herself. Such a valuable and practical guide for companioning a young person!"
—**Sherrill Knezel**, visual thinking strategist

"*The Power of Natural Mentoring* draws on stories from real women to emphasize today's critical need for caring adults to be present and involved in the lives of girls and younger women. The author explains natural mentoring in such a warm and caring manner, with data to back up her arguments. The last chapter's practical how-to guide is as helpful for adult women's self-development as it is for their girls. Highly recommend."
—**Kimichelle Bain**, women's transformation coach

"In my fourteen-year career as an early childhood education teacher, I had the great fortune to teach and learn from approximately three hundred teenage girls. A few weeks before each school year began, I felt a bit of anxiety and excitement about the challenges and opportunities these students presented. Would I be able to inspire them, as my favorite high school teacher inspired me? Could I make a real difference in their lives as they followed their dreams of teaching young children? I know that I *have* had a lasting, positive impact on some of the girls I've taught—but I wonder how many more I could have helped with a more intentional focus on mentoring.

I highly recommend *The Power of Natural Mentoring: Shaping the Future for Women and Girls* to help you reflect on your own values, talents, and lessons learned from life experiences that *you* can share with a girl or young woman facing many uncertainties, stresses, and decisions in life. I took notes as I read through the chapters. The book made me think back on people who influenced my own life.

Christine Wagner shares insightful interviews with women who've successfully mentored young girls and stories of young women who have benefited from having a natural mentor. Where to start? In this book you'll find helpful, research-based suggestions for beginning your natural mentoring journey. Are you ready to invest in the future?"
—**Jan Kennerknecht**, M.Ed.

"Christine Wagner understands and values the vital role mentors play in the lives of girls and young women. Although so many of tomorrow's women find themselves without the support they need to thrive, the women who are naturally in their lives—aunts, teachers, parents' friends—are too often unaware of the power they have to help. Christine reveals the capacity within each of us to engage with and support the young people in our lives as they strive to succeed."
—**TEDx** Albuquerque

THE POWER OF *Natural* MENTORING

THE
POWER
OF
Natural
MENTORING
Shaping the Future for Women and Girls

Christine G. Wagner

The Power of Natural Mentoring:
Shaping the Future for Women and Girls

Published by CWC Publishing
Albuquerque, New Mexico

Paperback ISBN: 978-1-7347527-0-0
eISBN: 978-1-7347527-1-7

Cover and Interior Design: GKS Creative
Copyediting and Proofreading: Kim Bookless
Editor: Megan Grennan
Illustrator: Sherrill Knezel
Project Management: The Cadence Group

To Emily

Heart of My Heart

Contents

Introduction

Is there a petunia in your life?

> Try thinking of families as gardens.
> If we arrive as a petunia in a garden of roses and lilies, we probably will need
> a friend, a neighbor, a teacher or a grandmother—someone who knows a
> petunia when she sees one and helps us bloom as ourselves.
> We need to make chosen families of small groups of women who support
> each other, talk to each other regularly, can speak their truths and their
> experiences, and find they're not alone in them. It makes all the difference.
> —Gloria Steinem[1]

Maybe *you* are a petunia. Think back and recall whether there was such a person in your life, someone who knew a petunia when she saw one. Someone who helped you bloom as yourself.

You probably didn't know it at the time, but that someone just may have been a natural mentor.

Despite increased opportunities for those of us who occupy half the planet, there is still no clear path to a fulfilling adult womanhood. Far too many girls and young women are struggling. They feel alone. We read or hear heartbreaking statistics daily in the news: Increased anxiety. Depression. Perfectionism. Bullying. Seclusion. To blossom into their true selves, girls need our attentive presence now more than ever before.

Women—and the girls and younger women we care deeply about—require *power* in order to thrive in today's uncertain world.

1

An instructor once asked my class what *power* meant to each of us. The responses reflected the fractured state of our world and were pretty negative: control, oppression, command, dominance, authority. To the last person, our minds went straight to *power over*—a show of force that demonstrates the polarity between weakness and strength.

But the kind of power required in today's world is distinctly different. It is the kind that best illustrates the origin of the word, from the Latin *potere*, meaning "to be able." This power means capacity, capability—a person's ability to do, to accomplish, to act in the world and to make things happen.

This is *power to*, and it comes from deep inside. It influences, energizes, and inspires confidence within us. Adult women have worked hard and are *still* working hard to cultivate this kind of power within ourselves over time. Our "deep inside" power strengthens the capacity to nurture *"power to"* within the girls and young women who are in our lives.

The caring capacity or *power to* walk with a girl or young woman on her life journey is called natural mentoring. I wrote this book to introduce you to the power and potential of this type of mentoring for girls in every kind of family garden—through the stories of real women living in today's world. These women wholeheartedly answered my call to speak with them about their experiences. They are either natural mentors themselves or may have been mentored at some points in their lives. Many have experienced both sides of mentoring. Because they personally lived the value of mentoring in their own lives, they wanted to give back. They made the decision to mentor someone else.

Every adult woman can be a natural mentor. You probably already are! Each of us has relationships with girls and young women who are present in our lives: our students, our nieces, our granddaughters, our friends' daughters, our younger colleagues, our neighbors. We have the power to intentionally deepen relationships with one or more of these girls and young women. We have the capacity to build networks of caring adults around them that research tells us they need in order to truly thrive.

Many women doubt they have the capacity to fill this role. Although natural mentoring is not a new idea, it is not known or fully understood by most of us. We can start by considering what it means not just to live but to thrive. Think flourishing health, vigorous growth, increasing strength, and positive development. The more we cultivate these aspects of ourselves in our everyday living, the greater our capacity to bring them forward in young people we care about.

This two-way cultivation is the aim of the book you hold in your hands. I am a lifelong learner and educator. My adult life began with teaching children, progressed to teaching and working with adults in graduate school and corporate America, and is culminating with a burning desire to fuse what I've learned to help women and girls thrive through natural mentoring relationships.

I think of thriving as a cycle with five components that are explored in depth in chapters 2 through 6 of this book. The first of these is *self-awareness*, not generally taught in schools but essential to expansive growth and development. Next comes a working knowledge of *brain development* and the new learning in neuroscience made possible by technologies like the fMRI that allow us to see inside a living brain to learn what is taking place there. With those two foundational areas under our belts, we are ready to examine the multiple changes taking place in our physical and inner lives, as well as in the world around us. When we learn that many *change experiences* can be intentionally navigated through the *process of transition*, we can step back and work through the challenges of changing with a clearer picture of our desired outcomes. In participating in the first three components of thriving, we are *leading from the inside out*, recognizing that to lead others, it is essential to lead ourselves first. Finally, we identify values that serve as measuring sticks for our actions and behavior—and begin to discover and use our *authentic voice* in the world to make whatever contributions we are here to make.

No one could possibly have captured the Thrive Cycle components more beautifully or precisely than my educator-illustrator-friend Sherrill Knezel, a heart-centered and eminently talented woman. Below is her wonderful drawing.

So, with great respect and even greater anticipation, I urge and invite you to delve into your capacity to deepen your relationship with a girl or young woman in your life through the pages of this book. If you doubt for a moment your *power to* be a presence in her life, to make a difference, to do meaningful work that will be returned to you many times over, think again. She *needs* your presence in her life. The world needs her voice. Be part of building a network of caring adults around her to enable her to thrive. In the process, you will recognize yourself and your power in each of the Thrive Cycle components.

Welcome to yourself. Welcome to helping her bloom as herself.

CHAPTER 1

Natural Mentoring

An Invitation

It's easy to fall in love with the GPS version of the universe.

There, just ahead, after that curve. Drive a little further, your destination is almost here.

Done. You've arrived.

Of course, that's not how it works. Not our careers, not our relationships, not our lives.

You've always arrived. You've never arrived.

Wherever you go, there you are. You're never going to arrive because you're already there.

There's no division between the painful going and the joyous arriving. If we let it, the going can be the joyful part.

It turns out that arrival isn't the point. It can't be, because we spend all our time on the journey.

—Seth Godin[1]

True confession: it took me a while to figure out there is no GPS for life. I still feel the intensely powerful emotions of young girlhood, adulthood approaching rapidly in hindsight yet far too slowly in the heat of the moment.

Can you recall those emotions? Do we ever forget them?

Somehow, girlhood passed: that exhilarating yet terrifying journey of growth, with its frustrating forks in the road, thorny questions, and crucial decisions to make. Despite endless-seeming days, the years accumulated swiftly. I became a woman.

Our collective experiences (the best, the worst, the ridiculous, the sad) form the lens we use to observe adolescent girls today. These girls are incredibly strong and innocently, wisely, beautifully young. We watch them embark on their own life journeys, coming of age in a bewildering, frightening, yet exciting and fascinating world.

Courageously facing its stunning complexities, they are members of the generation that will change that world, one way or another.[2]

Despite extraordinary opportunities for girls and their future, they face unprecedented risk. The CDC reports suicide rates for fifteen- to nineteen-year-old girls have doubled since 2007, reached a forty-year high in 2015, and continue to grow.[3] Girls who spend the most time using technology are five times more likely to say they are sad or depressed every day.[4] In alignment with this statistic, nearly three times as many girls as boys will have their first experience with depression between the ages of twelve and seventeen.[5] Even with the many and varied ways to connect, more than 40 percent of young people feel lonely today.[6]

What do we do to help our girls and young women?

An answer to this question lies within us, the significant adults in their lives.

Girls are far from alone on their life journeys. It is up to us to support their success. Our girls are the witnesses beside us. They are watching the ways we approach living in uncertain and unprecedented times.

They are following our uncharted paths with interest and curiosity.

They see our struggles to pinpoint and utilize our full potential. They observe our steps forward and back. They notice when we summon the strength to rise again after we fall. They appreciate the courageous and authentic work we do in our effort to make a difference in a world in transition. They may laugh at our lack of technology finesse, but they also cheer us on and joyfully celebrate our successes.

Girls may be frightened of the adult doors opening to them. They face challenges we never considered. At the same time, they are on the brink of their own brilliance. As adult women, we have an urgent opportunity to positively impact their lives.

Who are these girls?

They are the girls of our hearts: our daughters and nieces, our friends' daughters and our daughters' friends, our students and our granddaughters.

This is an invitation for all women to provide
a critical growth and support network for girls.

We are here to mirror the beauty of their uniqueness. Our close relationships with adolescent girls can teach them to see themselves in the most positive light, as they find and speak their voice and identify their talents and gifts, as they determine how to use them for good.

We are their natural mentors, the caring adults who choose to make a difference in the life of a young person.

The time has come to fine-tune this role, because our girls need us, and the future needs them.

Close your eyes and envision women and girls making their life journeys together, deepening their relationships, and supporting each other.

Together, we will transform the world.

Who was your mentor?

And the day came
when the risk
to remain tight
in a bud
was more painful
than the risk
it took
to blossom.
—Anais Nin

The significance of mentors in the lives of girls cannot be overstated. Research outcomes on resiliency at the Center on the Developing Child at Harvard tell us that despite hardship and adversity, the single most common factor for young people who do well is *having the support of at least one stable and committed relationship with a caring adult.*[7] A network of positive relationships impacts the life of a young person even more.[8]

This was reinforced for me a few years ago at a gathering of selected high-performing women from a national direct sales company. The after-dinner meeting I'd been asked to facilitate was just beginning.

My eyes slowly scanned the intent faces around the circle of tables. Twenty-four women sat lost in thought, silently memory surfing over a question I'd just asked. In a few minutes, each would introduce herself and tell a story from her own life.

"Who was your mentor?"

Introductions began and one by one, mentor stories poured out. There were halting accounts of beloved grandmothers who supported and loved unconditionally. Then came laugh-out-loud descriptions of awesome aunts who somehow "got" a young woman's "strange" personality. And the stories kept coming: teachers who taught much more than school subjects; sports coaches whose roles far surpassed sports; work colleagues and managers who nurtured the women as they developed the workers. One or two couldn't remember having a mentor but explained that parents had filled the role.

Emotions overflowed. There were tears. As they spoke, many women in the room realized that well-deserved thanks had never been delivered to mentors who had made a real difference in their lives. They resolved aloud to do something about that.

This is a book about such mentors.

These essential adults can be described by the term "natural mentor." Unlike formal programs that match women with girls to build potential mentoring relationships, natural mentoring can happen with two people who are already (naturally) in each other's lives.

Today, more than ever, girls and young women require caring adults in their lives to thrive. The world seems to be shaking beneath us. Can you feel the uncertainty? We need stamina, strength, and courage to navigate the complexity of the changes. To do that, we must know ourselves deeply and support each other's growth generously.

The women and girls whose stories you will read came forward voluntarily—and eagerly!—to tell them. As you read, I invite you to remember a woman in your life.

Who was your mentor? You may not have thought of her as a mentor at the time. How did this woman impact your life? Is she still here? Still making the difference only she can make? Maybe there were multiple women. How might your life be different today if they had not so willingly shared theirs with you?

To begin, let me tell you a story of my own.

Who Was My Mentor?

On a warm spring day, the halls of my high school were crackling with the prospect of summer vacation. As junior and senior classes snaked into an already-crammed auditorium for Honors Assembly, I scanned the rafters, wondering about the crowd seated up there. Parents! Of course. Newly elected National Honor Society members would be announced today, and their parents had been secretly invited to the assembly.

My expectations were not very high. It was the end of my junior year, and I understood the caliber of student who might be elected to NHS as a junior. Although I was a good student and an active one, somehow I hadn't considered the possibility . . . until I caught sight of those parents.

There they were! My mom and dad, seated up in the rafters. Surprise—and a little disbelief—shivered through me. It dawned on me that teachers and administrators in my high school regarded *me* as NHS material. As a junior? Really?

The next day at another assembly, the words of our superintendent seared through me. "You . . ." his eyes swept the faces in the room, "are the cream of the crop. Your success in high school has created your blueprint for the future. Whatever you decide to do with your life, you have demonstrated the skills and determination to achieve. This is a tribute to your families. It is a tribute to you, too, and it is also a tremendous responsibility. So, choose wisely. Be a force for good. You have the potential to change the world!"

Happiness and pride coursed through me. Then, as the words settled in, I realized there was another emotion mixed in there too.

FEAR.

In my mind, the big question that loomed large, was HOW? How would I choose that "whatever"—that thing I would decide to do with my life?

Who would help me? I am the oldest of four siblings, so my parents were supportive and encouraging but inexperienced at coaching a soon-to-be college freshman on her life direction. How would I choose a path among the bewildering array of professions and career options? Who—and what—did I want to be? I felt uneasy, inept, and utterly ill-equipped with either the self-awareness or the career-awareness to choose *anything*, much less choose wisely.

I remember that sixteen-year-old feeling of fearful ineptitude like it was yesterday. I felt completely alone. It sure didn't feel like I was "the cream of the crop." I wished for someone— anyone—to take an interest in me and work with me to find a direction for my life's path.

Wasn't there a roadmap for life somewhere?

And who was *my* mentor?

I loved hanging out with children, so I became a teacher. In the suburban school district where I taught fourth grade, there were programs for children with special needs, children who were "talented and gifted" and "at risk," the behaviorally challenged, those diagnosed with ADHD. Often, as I sat in front of empty desks in my classroom during late afternoon paper grading sessions, I thought about the other students, especially the girls, who didn't fit in any of the existing program categories. Those who, like me, followed the rules and listened to directions. They did all their homework and got good grades. They made friends and navigated the social networks of the playground. Yet I often wondered about their self-discovery process. Who would help *them* to launch a meaningful and purposeful life path?

Later, in the early 2000s, my career had shifted from teaching children to workforce development. I joined a visioning team tasked with creating an executive MBA program designed to meet the employment needs of the local business community. When the program began, I taught what the students considered breakthrough introductory courses because of the personal introspection required.

Through assessments and research, the MBA students explored the kind of self-discovery most had never experienced before. They learned about the brain and the implications of their unique thinking, communication, and learning preferences. They identified their values, strengths, and weaknesses. They rated their emotional intelligence. Then students carefully analyzed this new learning about themselves. They wrote a personal effectiveness plan with specific strategies to follow on the road to graduation—strategies that included outcomes to lead them in the direction of their chosen life and career goals.

For many, the resulting self-awareness was life changing. One student sent me a victory email:

> *It was a really valuable learning process about just who I am and what I am about. I feel as though I have found a spot in life to operate from and go forward—been looking for it for a long time. I went through three hours of parent-teacher conferences last night and realized I'm so much more in touch with myself, my children, my life.*

Why, I wondered in frustration, was *graduate school* the first time these learners looked purposefully inward toward self-discovery? Shouldn't this self-directed study have begun much earlier in their lives?

All this internal mulling came to a head for me during heart-to-heart conversations at a women's retreat in Chicago in 2010. I looked around at engaged and animated faces and suddenly found myself wishing each of us had a young high schooler or college woman by her side. What powerful life and business stories were being exchanged, and what rich learning could take place with young women and girls among us!

I went home and Googled "mentoring." Then I focused on women and girls. After scrolling through thousands of hits, one thing was certain. More than ever before, women and girls are called upon to bring out the best in each other. There is a critical need for women to support each other and walk beside the next generation of women who will lead the world.

During the early 2000s, adolescent girls began disconnecting from themselves and others. They went into a "crisis mode" of behaviors such as too-early emphasis on "looking sexy," overuse of social media, and self-harming resulting from anxiety.[9] The American Psychological Association called for "hardiness zones" where caring adults actively engage with adolescent girls on their journey to adulthood.[10] The Search Institute's research identified a "team of caring adults" in teens' lives as not only a good thing, *but necessary for the teens to thrive.*[11] The research also noted that only one in five teens in the United States has more than one caring adult. Many do not have one.

The difference can be made by women like you and me. Mentors are women who influence, inspire, love, and guide younger women and girls. These women see strengths in others because they are strong. They recognize the capacity for leadership because they are leaders. They inspire self-awareness because they value self-knowledge.

Through my research, I learned of another, more frequent kind of mentoring than programs that formally match young people with adults. It is called *natural mentoring* because it occurs between pairs of adults and young people who are naturally in each others' lives, like relatives, friends' children, students, or church acquaintances. Some cultures call these caring adults "other mothers." *This* was a concept all women could embrace!

The Power of Natural Mentoring

A picture began to form in my head of what adolescence could look like for girls if more women stepped up and became active participants in the girls' lives. Adult women had already experienced many of the "usual" developmental changes girls face as they journey to adulthood. Remarkably, today's women also are experiencing unique changes in a world growing more unpredictable and uncertain.

In mentorship, relationship, and partnership, what if women and girls developed strategies together to intentionally transition through the changes? By increasing their self-awareness, perhaps those strategies could build on each other, resulting in a uniquely personal GPS for the journey of life. Instead of a global positioning system, it would be an *inner* GPS, coming straight from the heart. That was an idea with potential!

I began to talk about natural mentoring to anyone who would listen. Women and girls not only listened, they offered suggestions, names, organizations, and enthusiastic encouragement. I learned women were willing but somewhat fearful and a bit unsure of what they had to offer in their capacity to mentor young girls.

I read countless books about aspects of adolescence, many of which are referenced as resources in the Notes and Bibliography sections at the end of this book. After gathering input from a group of twelve interested women in Columbus, Ohio, as initial advisors, Power2Thrive, a program that brings girls and women together in natural mentoring relationships, began taking shape.

Encouraged by enthusiastically positive feedback from my MBA students, I decided to build on self-awareness and leadership from the inside out. My consulting work with businesses in forming effective teams confirmed the value of opening the eyes of adults to their inner selves, their strengths and values, and working to close the gap between their current selves and their highest future selves.

The program I envisioned has two parts. The first part consists of workshops for adult women who want to learn more about themselves, build their natural mentoring capacity, and deepen a relationship with a girl who is already in their life. She could be a young friend or colleague, a student, a niece, a granddaughter . . . there are many possibilities. These workshops are designed to build on the women's current self-awareness, identify and confirm their gifts, and assist them with a toolkit of approaches for intentionally engaging adolescents in safe relationships of trust.

The second part of the program includes workshops for the women and girls together. Natural mentors introduce their girls to the meaning of leadership from the inside out, equipping them with the self-awareness to begin identifying their own strengths and values to help them determine the highest self they aspire to be as adults. Together, they strategize a uniquely personal GPS journey to adulthood.

As part of the journey, the pairs identify a concrete project to work on together to solve a problem in an area of interest to both. Through this "field experience," the women accompany the girls in taking an idea to a solid conclusion. This is a way to connect and stay connected, deepening their relationship as they moved forward.

The women and girls agree to five purposes together:

- Commitment to each other
- Commitment to a sustained, long-term, meaningful relationship
- Face-to-face meetings and fun activities
- Productive conversations grounded in trust
- The give-and-take of caring and emotional attachment

I introduce natural mentoring's essence and spirit and the Power-2Thrive program concepts in the remaining chapters of this book through the amazing life stories of actual women and girls in natural mentoring relationships. These are the wonderful women who enthusiastically answered my call to be interviewed and to tell their stories. Many initiated contact with me after hearing about my work from other participants.

It was important to me to introduce the natural mentoring concepts through real-life experiences. I let out the word to colleagues and friends that I was looking for women to interview who had mentored or been mentored. Then the project took on a life of its own. After interviewing more than fifty women who came forward through word of mouth, I realized the interviews could probably continue indefinitely. Not one woman refused to tell her story.

Marie and Katrina were the first two women to sit down in conversation with me. I was initially struck by their polar opposite experiences. Each one's story aptly illustrates the impact—or lack—of a caring adult in her life.

When she was seven, Marie woke up one morning and discovered her hair all over the pillow beneath her head. She'd been slogging through a bitter divorce with her parents, and the stress of the family's painful experience caused her to lose every strand overnight. If that wasn't bad enough, Marie's elementary school's strict "no hats" rule forced her to endure the startled looks and sidelong comments of her classmates that day and the days that followed.

The events in Marie's life could have led to an emotional and behavioral downward spiral. Instead, Marie's suffering marked the start of an enduring relationship. Her mother's best friend, Stephanie, stepped in. She began meeting Marie at school and walking home with her. She made dates with Marie and took her to movies. Time and again, Stephanie demonstrated that someone consistently cared and would be there to listen when Marie wanted to talk or vent.

They celebrated Marie's eighth birthday together by going out for ice cream. The close relationship and the ice cream tradition continued through college. Stephanie became Marie's go-to person on phone calls from school and during school breaks throughout college. When Marie began her career, she reversed the honor and began taking Stephanie out for ice cream on *her* birthday.

In stark contrast, Katrina's traumatic life event led to a different outcome. Her best friend, her older sister, was killed in a car accident while she was in high school.

I wish a natural mentoring program was available to me when I was younger. I see the value of natural mentors to young girls, and it almost makes me wonder why I never reached out to my own natural mentors after my older sister was killed when I was thirteen. Then again, it makes me wonder even more why my natural mentors didn't reach out to me! I lost the one natural mentor that I was closest to—the one I was influenced by, the one I looked up to. And when that happened, I went from being popular to being antisocial because I didn't know how to cope. I went from being very confident in myself to not believing I had any self-worth. I went from being extremely healthy and active to battling two eating disorders for over a decade.

The chapters of this book introduce each component in the Thrive Cycle. This cycle applies to both mentors and their girls or young women, and each chapter is aligned with corresponding experiential learning that takes place in the activities of the Power2Thrive natural mentoring program. They form a toolkit of resources for pairs of women and girls to thrive as they enhance their own natural mentoring relationships.

Thrive Cycle

- Becoming "Whole Self" Aware
  –the blossoming and nurturing of aspects of the self
- Becoming "Whole Brain" Aware
  –the interpersonal neurobiology of connections
- Celebrating Change
  –intentionally experiencing change as a process of transition
- Leading from the Inside Out
  –developing talents, strengths, and nurturing leadership
- Finding and Using My Voice
  –identifying values that inform and inspire my voice

Moms, Dads, and Guardians: Team Captains

Most important, a word or two about moms, dads, and guardians. Research outcomes that inform us every young person needs a team of caring adults to thrive place moms and dads hands down as captains of the team.[12] As your beloved daughter matures, she needs you more than ever but in different ways. She is beginning a critical separation process toward independent adulthood. It may appear she is growing apart from you.[13]

Nothing could be further from the truth. As she moves by trial and error toward the independence she understands will be expected of her as an adult, ongoing research of teens tells us they are *asking* for our presence in their lives, in real time, face to face.[14]

Your daughter also requires the perspective of other adults, role models who can open her mind and heart to herself through the lens of their life experiences and caring expertise. It is up to you to trust in your parental love, to monitor and encourage these relationships in their potential to significantly enhance your daughter's journey to adulthood.

A bonus (and research-based) benefit for teens who have a relationship with caring adult(s) outside their home is they are more likely to talk with their parents about "things that really matter."[15] Yay!

A final, important aside: of course, boys need natural mentors too. I began this work with girls because I know them best. Dads, uncles, older brothers, cousins, grandfathers, teachers, coaches—all men—here's a question for you: *Who was your mentor?*

Your Invitation

In my teen years, I longed for someone to walk beside me in the decision-making processes of my life. I knew my parents loved me, but I needed other adults to help me answer big questions that could take me beyond the self that was forming inside to the Self—with a capital S—that I could become.

I needed a natural mentor. I needed an adult or adults who would commit to deepening our relationship and help me navigate my GPS for life.

So, this book is a heartfelt invitation. Use it to increase your self-awareness and gain supreme confidence in your capacity to mentor that young woman or girl in your life. And here's a secret: Your young woman or girl? Regardless of how much you may role model, teach, and influence, I guarantee you'll learn even more from her.

CHAPTER 2

Who Am I?

Examining the "Whole Self"

> Don't worry if you make waves
> simply by being yourself . . .
> The moon does it all the time.
> —Scott Stabile

Becoming self-aware is the first component of the Thrive Cycle—a lifelong process of examining and coming to know your whole self, feelings and emotions on the inside as well as actions and behaviors on the outside. It's turning on the GPS of your life for the first time, peering inside, and scrutinizing what's there.

Wouldn't you have loved (or if you were one of the lucky ones, maybe you had) a woman to take her place beside you when you were fifteen or sixteen—who truly listened when you needed to talk; believed in you; explored your creativity together and encouraged you to step into your strengths; trusted you to use your voice and make things happen?

Who are you? What makes you "you"? There are many ways to think of your whole self. It may be useful to define some of the key words and more prevalent aspects of the self.

Authentic self: the "real or true you" that is consistent with your values and behavior; the "you" at your center or core that motivates you to say and do what you think and feel.[1]

Mental models: beliefs and assumptions about how you view the world and act in it.

Mindset: awareness of your existing mental models, beliefs, and assumptions. A fixed mindset is the belief that intelligence or talents are fixed, unchangeable traits. A growth mindset is the belief that learning can occur and abilities can be developed through dedication and hard work.[2]

Self-awareness: the ability to understand what drives your emotions, to perceive your internal states, preferences, resources, and intuitions. It is a cornerstone of emotional intelligence.[3]

Self-concept: the perceptions, beliefs, and evaluations you have about yourself.

Self-esteem: an overall sense of your value or worth.

Self-efficacy: the belief in your capacity to successfully perform and influence events that affect your life.

Self-regulation: the ability to control your emotions and impulses.

Self-mastery: having a vision for your future self and actualizing your potential.

In this chapter, we explore self-awareness, a key skill to encourage and cultivate beginning in adolescence and continuing throughout life. Thinking about my own youthful self-scrutiny brought me back to another high school "evolving self" memory.

Beginning Self-Awareness

When I was in my teens, one of my favorite activities was a sleepover, especially if there were several of us together for the night. Contrary to its name, anyone who has ever been a teenager knows these events rarely included sleep. Instead, my friends and I lounged comfortably around the room talking. Nose to nose, hearts open, we revealed the secrets of our souls to each other. Ideas, dreams, fears, and hopes spilled out— and through the give and take of warm, intense, open dialog and laughter, we learned about ourselves. We listened, con- tributed, revised our thinking, and listened some more. In the morning, we left, hopefully even closer friends and definitely more self-aware than we had been the night before.

The ability to monitor our emotions and thoughts as we experience them is basic to understanding ourselves better, being content with who we are, and managing those thoughts, emotions, and behaviors. Self-awareness helps us achieve wholeness by balancing our energy along the GPS for life journey. It includes developing and integrating the four dimensions of our human "self"—physical, mental, emotional, and spiritual. Knowing who you are and how you impact others informs how you see, feel, think, and value yourself. Self-awareness is one of the first aspects of your self-concept to emerge and is a foundation for the leadership skills needed in today's uncertain world.

23

To assist you in better knowing yourself as a woman and natural mentor, we will closely examine three aspects of the self that work together in forming your world view and how you show up in the world: *self-concept, self-efficacy,* and *self-mastery.* You may not have thought about or considered the many aspects of self that make up who you are. As you delve into each of them, you are deepening your own self-awareness. At the same time, you are increasing your capacity to awaken self-awareness in your girl or young woman.

Finally, we will unpack how mental models and mindset affect not only your ways of seeing the world but your overall well-being. These concepts are not only useful for your adult path, they are valuable concepts that you can help your young woman or girl absorb and assimilate on her GPS journey.

A Natural Mentor's GPS: Starting the Journey

Adults are role models for children. As such, their very presence reveals the essence of the adult "self" to the young people in their lives. Caring adults—parents, teachers, relatives, and coaches—have the capacity to assist girls to thrive: to deeply know and understand themselves physically, mentally, emotionally, and spiritually.

As adults consider mentoring, some serious soul-searching often occurs. How could I be a mentor? What do I have to offer a young girl? (And what in the world do I do when she rolls her eyes at me?)

If you're asking yourself these and other questions, you are engaging in "pre-mentor thinking." Directing this thinking with attention and intention serves two purposes. It equips the prospective mentor with her own level of self-awareness. It then uncovers some important gifts a caring adult can offer a young girl. In formal mentoring programs that "match" mentors with youth, evidence-based "elements of effective practice" inform the mentors of what to do in the stages of a formal mentoring relationship.[4] Mentor training is one evidence-based element that builds a woman's self-efficacy in the beginning stages of formal mentoring.

In natural mentoring, you deeply care about a girl or young woman who is *already (naturally) present* in your life. This book is "natural mentor training"—a resource for you in bolstering your self-efficacy as you further develop this relationship that is already important to you both. You will come to realize and embrace your capacity for natural mentoring success in your relationship and as a positive influence in her life. You can do this!

Considering your motives, goals, and expectations is a good place to start in deepening the relationship you have with your girl or young woman. This book can help you identify goals for yourself as a natural mentor. You can share your goals in conversation with your girl, requesting her to think about her own goals for herself and the relationship with you. Comparing your mentoring goals with your girl's goals enables the two of you to pinpoint and address any discrepancies between them. Together you can synchronize and manage your expectations for the continuing relationship.

Once you both have agreed that taking your relationship to a deeper level is something you want to do, take time for several good, honest, heart-to-heart conversations. Soul search with each other about what comes next. The questions below can be excellent conversation starters from both the adult's and the girl's perspective. Go out for lunch together and have another talk. Take a long, leisurely hike in nature together and continue the conversation further. Make time and space to listen to each other at separate intervals and let things sink in during times apart.

Ten questions below may be helpful in getting started with sharing conversations. There are at least three ways the questions can be used. First, your own adult responses to the questions can help in sorting out the many aspects of self a woman has worked hard on and refined in her life, qualities she can model as she assists a young person to begin developing self-awareness. Assessing these aspects of the adult self can be helpful in beginning the GPS journey of a natural mentor.

Second, a girl's responses to many of these questions can reveal fundamental features of the essential "self" she is striving to be. Over time, they can facilitate an adolescent to form an ideal image of her possible adult "Self" and, with the help, support, and love of the caring adults around her, begin to envision a GPS for her life—a roadmap for the journey.

Third, the two of you can share your responses with each other as a way to learn more about each one's experiences, perspective, thoughts, and feelings. (Later in this book, we will delve into many of the important concepts in these questions, like change and transitions, strengths, leadership, values, and voice.)

- What about mentoring (or being mentored) appeals to me?
- Who am I? (How do I deal with my emotions? How do I think and behave in the world? What personality traits do I embody?)
- What are my strengths? My weaknesses?
- What are my most important values?
- What life changes have I navigated successfully / not so successfully?

- What life transitions am I currently experiencing?
- What life lessons have I learned (am I learning now)?
- What is my leadership style? Do I have one? How can I develop a style that fits me if I don't already have one?
- How do I express my essential or authentic self?
- How do I use my voice in the world?

As an adult, you can also draw from some or all of the prompts below to help your girl begin to know you better. There may be other prompts or questions you can think of that do not appear on this list that apply to the two of you. By thoughtfully considering her natural mentor's responses, a girl can begin her own self-exploration. She may be hearing many of these concepts for the first time. A natural mentor can listen and respond thoughtfully to questions her girl may ask. Here are some possibilities:

- What causes me to do the things I do, think and reason clearly or not, experience the feelings that are inside, and say the words that bubble up and pop out of my mouth?
- What do all these inform me about my inner thoughts, my values, beliefs, personality?
- What does it mean to be aware? (Besides knowing, awareness is *noticing*: picking up on cues or signals that I recognize and can name.)
- After noticing, what does a person do with this information?
- How does awareness enhance or improve life?
- What can I do with what I notice that will increase my self-awareness?
- As I notice more and more—like patterns of behavior that emerge over time—what can I learn from the patterns that will make my life easier or better?

Despite its importance, becoming self-aware is not usually taught in mainstream school until graduate school—if then. There is a critical opportunity for natural mentors to help fill this gap.

As a natural mentor, the greatest gifts you can give your girl are a safe space to talk, trust that goes both ways, and then to actively listen. She may be wondering so many things but unable or even afraid to articulate her feelings. Inside her head, it may sound a little like this:

What is going on with me? Who is my Self, with a capital S—the best form of "me" I can be? What is a self, anyway? Are a person's inner and outer self the same? Are they supposed to be the same? What if they aren't?

There are so many MEs! There's the voice in my head that thinks constantly. Sometimes I want to turn it off and make it go away. There's the me that feels feelings intensely, whether they're happy or sad, good or bad. There's also the me deep inside, the real, true me, that may be afraid to be revealed. Maybe that 'real me' won't be accepted, won't be the me that gets and keeps friends, that has a place in my family, my classroom, my crowd. Which of these selves is the one I want to be, anyway? What aspects of myself do I love and respect in other people, like my family, friends, my natural mentor? Can I create my own self? If the answer to that question is yes, how do I make that happen?

What makes me feel certain feelings? What situations that I find myself in cause me to shut down and want to hide? What situations or experiences bring me alive, open my heart, help me to see myself and others more clearly?

When small children act and react, they are unaware of their inner selves and what is happening behind the scenes inside the body. As they grow and learn to recognize patterns of behavior, they repeat actions that work on their behalf. Saying "thank you" may result in a hug, signifying Mom or Dad's approval. This feels wonderful, so they do it again and again. The glimmers of self-awareness are born and so are qualities such as kindness and courtesy.

But what happens when they are frustrated, angry, sad, confused—how do they convey these emotions that arise during the experience of daily living? As children accumulate more self-awareness, they begin to recognize the events and people that trigger a variety of emotions within them. When they are aware of their triggers, they can learn ways to moderate their reactions and choose their responses. Chapter 3 shines a light on the intense emotions that are hallmarks of adolescence. There is a physical reason for girls' volatility and difficulty with self-regulation. The adolescent brain is growing and, in the process, it is undergoing some major preparation for adulthood.

The following story illustrates the profound impact a natural mentor can have on a teen girl's life and the mutually satisfying growth both adult and girl can experience in their self-awareness and in deep relationship with one another. I emailed my colleague and friend Jane, telling her of my intention to write this book and requesting her to send me names of women she might know who had been mentored or mentors themselves. She immediately let me know she had mentored several students and couldn't wait to tell me about Kathie. In return, Kathie eagerly talked with me about the meaningful relationship she and Jane had sustained for the past twenty years.

Jane and Kathie: A Story of Self-Awareness

She gave me direction without giving me directions. She almost gave me a light at the end of the tunnel. I think she made me realize what I could look like as an adult.

Teachers—and all adults connected with education—have firsthand opportunities to be natural mentors. Jane K. saw a glimmer in fifteen-year-old Kathie B. Their relationship increased Kathie's confidence and provided supportive direction in discovering and exploring her gift of teaching young children:

I was teaching a three-year childcare program to high school students. Kathie was with me more than two and a half hours a day, five days a week, for three years. That's a lot of time. She was a real high-flyer, very positive person, very good with the children in the preschool we ran three days a week. She kind of took a leadership position early on. She was my go-to person.

She was struggling, her mother was sick, the family couldn't really afford college—and so (after she enrolled) I did my best to help. I would hire her to help me, she'd come and we'd clean my house together on Saturdays, or she helped with some childcare. I just tried to encourage her to keep going and eventually . . . she dropped out because of finances. It was difficult.

I kind of lost touch with her then, for a few years, and recently reconnected with her on social media. We've [been chatting] and recently she stopped in with her two children and her husband and a baby she's adopting. She came in to tell me she's enrolling back in college again.

I think [our relationship] has been life mentoring, a nurturing relationship. I was trying to encourage her and let her know that she could do this and that she would do well. It was gratifying to me; hopefully it was helpful to her. She is just a very determined young woman, and I'm hoping that the praise I gave her, the positive feedback, the encouragement—it all kind of stayed in the back of her mind over the years and made her feel like she had a goal she wanted to achieve, and she did. She is going to achieve it.

And from Kathie's perspective: *She saved me.*

Kathie B's home life was messy. Her mom drank and her stepdad was abusive. Her friends were experimenting on the fringe and she was following them.

The tenth grader was, in her own words, lost.

Then she enrolled in a childcare class in her hometown's tech school. She knew one thing. She loved kids and she wanted to teach them. As Kathie puts it, she and the teacher in the class—Mrs. K.—had a connection from the beginning.

She really made me find my love for teaching. She just gave me the confidence that I never had in myself. I just never had a real strong female role model in my life, until that point. . . . She was such an awesome encourager. . . . It wasn't enough to make you nervous, push you, but it just gave me confidence in myself, that I knew that she was behind me one hundred percent.

Sometimes I'd find little notes, encouraging notes. 'I'm so proud of you. You know you can do this.'. . . There were times when I would have a hard time and I would go and I would talk to her about things. I knew she was there, just through little things she would say, little things she would do. . . . I never felt like there would be any negativity at all from her. Just this calmness about her and openness for me, that I never had with someone before, other than my grandmother. She was just the first person that I felt listened to me.

She was a loving mentor, but she was a very strong mentor for me as well. . . . I never had someone who saw something in me that I didn't see and push me towards it. That's how she gave me that confidence.

Mrs. K. encouraged Kathie to participate in a career skills competition. Kathie progressed, winning first place in the regional competitions and finally earning third place nationally.

She really helped me realize that I had a talent. I had a gift. She knew I had it in me and that I needed to step out of the box and show people what I knew. [The skills competition] was an amazing thing for me because it made me not be reserved.

She gave me direction without giving me directions. She almost gave me a light at the end of the tunnel. I think she made me realize what I could look like as an adult.

Valuable discoveries from the relationship with Mrs. K. reached beyond the classroom for Kathie.

You do dumb things in high school. Peer pressure was hard for me because I didn't fit in. In Mrs. K.'s class, I finally had a place where I belonged. I knew I was good there; I knew it was something I excelled at. That someone saw that I excelled at. It made me feel so great that I finally got self-confidence and was able to tell people no. I was able to stop hanging out with friends that I only hung out with because I wanted to be cool. They weren't good friends.

I wanted to be myself and figure out who 'myself' was. I realized, when you're good at something and when you have people that care about you and are pushing for you—you know, rooting for you and on your side—you don't have to be afraid to be who you are because even if you do something wrong and you fail at something, they still love you. I don't think I knew that, before Mrs. K.

The relationship between Kathie and Mrs. K. has ebbed and flowed more than twenty years. When Kathie went to college after three years in Mrs. K.'s class, finances were a serious issue for her. Mrs. K. hired her to clean her house and be a nanny for her children. Kathie never graduated but has recently enrolled at a local university to continue her education. Mostly on social media now, she and Mrs. K. plan her strategy together and stay connected.

Even twenty years later, I'm going back to school in the fall. I know what I want and how I want to do it. That all started with her. She planted that seed.

I hope that I was able to touch her life; even just a small amount would suffice for me. If it's even a percentage of how much she affected my life and my story . . . she is such a huge chapter of my life that I just certainly hope I was able to do the same for her.

Authentic Self and Social Self: Is There a Difference?

Natural mentoring provides an opportunity to examine and assess the quality of how adult women live their lives. Does what you do reflect who you are at your core? Or is your pattern of behavior like the chameleon, changing to fit in with the group you happen to be involved with at the time? What do we know about authenticity, and why is it important for girls to witness a caring adult who models living an authentic life?

Authentic self is the "real or true you" that is consistent with your values and behavior, the "you" at your center or core who says and does what you truly think and feel. Who among us has not adjusted her personality to suit an occasion, a group, or a place? Remaining authentic while adjusting your social self to the context of the situation is key. The danger lies in becoming so immersed in those around you that you lose yourself in striving to fit in.

Authenticity is an important positive psychology concept, and research links it to well-being. Most encouraging of all, it is possible to increase our levels of feeling and behaving authentically.[5]

Becoming authentic is a continuous, lifelong process along the GPS journey for both natural mentor and young woman or girl. Becoming authentic means accepting and continuously improving who you are, personal faults and failures as well. Besides knowing who you are at your core, it involves cultivating authentic relationships and cherishing their influence among individuals in the wider world.

Sense of Self

Some definitions at the beginning of this chapter highlight many aspects of a "whole self." Here, we concentrate on a broad view of your *sense of self*, the perceptions, beliefs, judgments, and feelings you have about yourself, as well as an adolescent's growing sense of self.

Acquainting yourself and the young woman or girl you mentor with the many aspects of the "whole self" can jump-start the GPS journey to self-awareness for her. It can also increase your own knowledge because you, too, are on a GPS journey, a personal path of self-awareness as a woman and as a natural mentor.

Self-concept and self-efficacy are components of a broad, overall sense of self. Self-mastery is the sought-after end result of a gap between your current self and your future self—the Self with a capital S—that you identify and aspire to be.

Self-concept contains the perceptions, beliefs, and evaluations you have about yourself. These include your beliefs about physical and mental characteristics, likes and dislikes, and strengths and weaknesses.

Your previous successful or unsuccessful performance, the performance and behaviors of others, and membership in groups with collective strengths and weaknesses can influence your self-concept.

Self-efficacy is the belief in your capacity to successfully perform and influence events that affect your life. Your self-efficacy plays a big part in how you approach goals, tasks, and challenges.

Your strong sense of self-efficacy helps you to:

- View challenging problems as tasks to be mastered
- Develop deeper interest in activities in which you participate
- Form a stronger sense of commitment to your interests and activities
- Recover quickly from setbacks and disappointments

Self-mastery is the ability to make the most out of your physical, mental, emotional, and physical health: to be the best you can be. It is having a vision for your future self and actualizing your potential. You can think of it like a rubber band between the "current you" and your "best Self" you—the vision you have of your highest Self in your future life. In this tension lies every possibility and potential you possess. This can be the most exciting aspect of the GPS journey for life.

The concepts in each of the chapters in this book progressively increase a natural mentor's self-knowledge as well as a growing understanding of the girl in your life. They are intended to assist you to incrementally strengthen your girl or young woman's ability to assess her current self. Armed with this new self-knowledge, she can begin to intentionally envision the journey to her adult Self. A natural mentor's goal is to provide safe spaces to actively listen and support the young woman or girl in her life in using her newly emerging self-awareness to identify her self with a capital S and consider what she can conceive and achieve in her adult life.

Authentic Listening

As you begin your natural mentoring relationship, your interest in each other will spark conversation. Your girl is hungry for the face-to-face connection that has become a rarity for many adolescents whose preferred form of communication is technology. The basis of meaningful conversation is *active and authentic listening*. This type of listening is more than hearing what someone is saying. It is listening with all of your senses. It is also listening from your heart. The Circle of Trust Touchstones are among the most authentic guidelines for creating a sacred space where you and your girl can feel safe to be yourselves and experience genuine dialog with one another.

- *Give and receive welcome.* Greet each other with genuine pleasure at being together in a hospitable space.
- *Be present as fully as possible.* Be open to being together with your doubts, fears, and failings, as well as your beliefs, joys, and successes. Be present with your listening as well as with your speaking.
- *What is offered when you are together is by invitation, not demand.* Your time with each other is not a "share or die" event. Each of you say and do what your soul calls for, and you say and do it with each other's support.
- *Speak your truth in ways that respect other people's—especially your girl's—truth.* Our views of reality may differ, but speaking one's truth when you are together does not mean interpreting, correcting, or debating what each other says. Speak from your center using "I" statements.
- *No fixing, saving, advising, or correcting each other.* This is one of the hardest guidelines when you want to help. It is vital to welcoming the inner teacher.
- *Learn to respond to each other with honest, open questions instead of counsel or corrections.* With such questions, we help "hear each other into deeper speaking."
- *When the going gets rough, turn to wonder.* If you feel judgmental or defensive, ask yourself: "I wonder what brought her to this belief?" "I wonder what she's feel-

ing right now?" "I wonder what this reaction teaches me about myself?" Set aside judgment to listen to her—and to yourself—more deeply.

- *Attend to your own inner teacher.* Pay close attention to your own reactions and responses, to your most important teacher.
- *Trust and learn from the silence.* Silence is a gift in our noisy world and a way of knowing in itself. After you or your girl speak, take time to reflect without immediately filling the space with words.
- *Observe deep confidentiality.* Nothing said in trust between you will ever be repeated to other people. Caveat: What about your responsibility to your girl or young woman's parents or guardian? This depends on her age and the level of concern you feel about something she has confided in you. Think of yourself as a parent or guardian. If you would need to know something your daughter has confided in a natural mentor, consider a discussion with your girl about the seriousness of the matter that leads her to understand it must be made known outside your close circle of trust. Encourage her to open up herself.
- Know that it is possible to leave each other with whatever you needed when you arrived together and that the seeds planted during your time together can keep growing in the days ahead.

Adapted with permission from the Center for Courage and Renewal, http://www.couragerenewal.org.[6]

Authentically listening during conversations with your girl or young woman can provide a safe space where she can sort out her young sense of self and begin to envision her place in the world. In the next section, I introduce two states of mind and a way of thinking that can make this journey to adulthood exciting and fruitful. Their influence is even greater in the presence of one or more caring adults whose authentic voice(s) can be counted on every step of the way.

Mental Models and Mindset

We do not see things as they are.
We see them as we are.
—Anais Nin

By exploring the ways our life experiences affect how we see the world, natural mentors can review the workings of their own minds in preparation for assisting your girls with this new learning. We all see the world through very different lenses. These personal lenses are made clearer by our life events: the family we were born into, our family's religious views and values, the schools we went to, the sports and other activities we participated in, the friends we keep company with, and the neighborhood, state, and country in which we live.

People construct *mental models* from the meaning we make of our experiences. Many times, we focus on certain aspects of an experience and ignore others. The movie of our life shows us data. We interpret and make meaning of that data through the lens of our life experiences, and then we conceptualize our often-skewed interpretation as "fact." The gap between our personal mental models and reality will increase over time until we test our assumptions, gather new data, and update our mental models. This requires intention, attention, and consistent effort.

The Ladder of Inference is a useful tool to help us understand how we think and sometimes reach faulty conclusions.[7] The metaphor of a ladder describes the thinking process we go through, usually without consciously realizing it, to get from "the facts" as we interpret them to a conclusion, belief, and the actions we take.

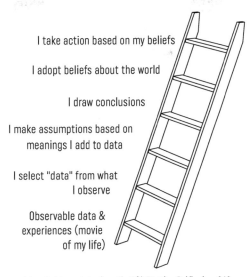

I take action based on my beliefs

I adopt beliefs about the world

I draw conclusions

I make assumptions based on meanings I add to data

I select "data" from what I observe

Observable data & experiences (movie of my life)

Adapted with permission from *The Fifth Discipline Fieldbook*, p. 243.

Natural mentors will want to consider their existing mental models, beliefs, and assumptions, also known as a person's mindset. Many mental models are the result of past learning experiences that may not have been reexamined or updated. Observing these allows us to see how the conclusions we have reached influenced our actions. If we choose, we can update or revise them to reflect our current circumstances and new learning.

Here is one way you can make the effort to explore your mindset:

Think of a life event that has occurred recently for you. Perhaps a friend cancelled a lunch date because of a previous meeting she had forgotten about. Your feelings were hurt by this cancellation.

You may have jumped to the conclusion that she didn't want to have lunch with you in the first place and the "previous meeting" was just an excuse. In fact, you may reach the conclusion that she is looking for a way to ease herself out of your friendship!

Using the Ladder of Inference to guide you, intentionally walk yourself up the Ladder and pay attention as you reflect on your assumptions and test them in reaching the conclusion that your friend "blew you off" when she cancelled your lunch date.

- Is the data you chose to examine accurate? How do you know this?
- What assumptions did you make about this experience?
- What measures did you take to validate these assumptions? If you took no measures, retrace your steps up the Ladder and attempt to validate the assumptions you made. For example, approach this friend and simply *ask her* what happened and actively listen to her response.
- Were the conclusions you made accurate and valid? Why or why not? Is it possible to revise your conclusions based on validated assumptions?

Following this example, when you are working through the Ladder of Inference with an experience from your girl or young woman's life, take similar steps to validate assumptions and reach conclusions. This can be a valuable learning experience for you both, one you will want to repeat often to continually hone the skill of testing assumptions and updating mental models.

The mental models we hold about ourselves can be limited or expanded by another specific and highly useful definition of *mindset*. It has to do with the way people perceive themselves and their abilities as learners. There are two ways to think about this.

People with a *fixed mindset* believe their intelligence or talent are fixed traits. They spend their time documenting their intelligence or talent instead of developing them. They also believe that talent alone (for example, "being smart") creates success—and because of their talent, the success should occur *without effort*.

People with a *growth mindset* believe their most basic abilities can be developed through dedication and hard work—brains and talent are just the starting point.[8] This view creates a love of learning and a resilience that is essential for great "Self with a capital S" accomplishment.

We learn and protect our own mindsets, and each of us has a mixture of growth and fixed mindsets. The good news is both adults and young people can cultivate a growth mindset. Be aware of your own mindset and the way you talk about abilities. In growth mindset language, effort, mistakes, and failure are all pathways to learning and success. Use the word "yet." I can't speak Spanish . . . yet. I can't use a potter's wheel . . . yet. When I learn and practice, I will. Challenge your girl to develop strategies and make progress toward something she values. Remember to praise her for her hard work, her persistence, and for learning from her mistakes.

Natural Mentoring Strategies

The process of becoming self-aware presents new ideas for girls and young women. They may have never heard of a "whole self," an "authentic self," or any of the ways of thinking about oneself. Mental models and mindset may also be new to them. "Trying on" these terms in conversation can be a starting point for a natural mentor to engage a girl or young woman.

1. As she gains familiarity with the many aspects of self, she may recognize ways she talks to herself. Remind her to exercise self-compassion: she is learning!

   • Ask open-ended questions that encourage her to think about her perceptions of herself, her mental models, and her mindset.

- When she tells you about events in her life, help her examine her assumptions using the Ladder of Inference. Do her mental models need updating? Do yours? Enlist each other's help in seeing the movie of your life from new and different perspectives.
- Recall and relay stories from your own life as you learned about yourself.

2. When you hear her engage in negative self-talk, gently call her attention to this. Ask how she could revise her statements to reflect a more positive self-concept.

3. Positive yet objective praise can go a long way to helping a girl or young woman see herself in a positive light. Look for opportunities to recognize and highlight her mature decisions, interests, and talents.

4. To encourage feelings of self-efficacy, engage in mutually interesting activities that demonstrate a girl or young woman can take an idea and execute it to a completed project. Does she notice community needs? Help her find ways to get involved.

5. Life is a constant opportunity to strive toward self-mastery. Take time to have conversations around what this means for a girl or young woman. What does it mean to her to be her "best Self"? She may not have any ideas at first. Keep at it. What does it mean to you? Tell her stories from your life.

6. Self-mastery begins with the awareness of the tension between "current you" and "best Self you." Awareness is followed by making choices among many options. Finally, taking action on a number of ideas can whittle down choices and help her begin to make solid decisions based on trial and error results.

SELF-MASTERY =
a. Awareness
b. Choice (discernment)
c. Action

Gabby and Linda: Encouraging Self-Awareness

A natural mentor's support demonstrates the caring presence required by a girl or young woman in becoming intentionally self-aware. Gabby's story illustrates how one mentor encouraged self-awareness and a growth mindset. Her words to Linda, the young woman in her life, were: *Failure grows you. If you stay still and stay stagnant, you're not going to move [forward].*

Linda was deep in the college application process. She became fearful and hesitated to choose the medical path she had prepared for in high school. Gabby asked her to think about the worst thing that could happen. Linda was concerned she might not get accepted into the college or program of her choice.

They had conversations about other majors she might think about if that happened. Linda said her two loves were nursing and teaching. Gabby relayed her own story and the many detours she took on her journey to owning her own business as a massage therapist. She had worked at a fitness center, then for a chiropractor, and finally branched into her own massage therapy practice. She took one step forward after the other. She said, *I kept discovering who I am, what I am here for, what makes me happy.*

Through many conversations over time, Gabby helped Linda with the self-awareness to understand it was okay and

43

preferable not to strive for perfection. Linda learned that failure experiences are excellent teaching and learning opportunities. Gabby role modeled the value of effort and hard work in reaching for a goal to a woman's or girl's sense of self, as well as her capacity to keep moving forward from "current me" to "best Self me."

Becoming self-aware is an intentional process of self-reflection. Natural mentors can support girls and young women to consider aspects of themselves in searching for productive ways to learn and grow their abilities, to align their feelings with their behavior. Understanding the many layers of self can help girls begin to answer questions they are asking at this stage in life—*Who am I?* and *Who will I be as an adult woman?* Growing self-awareness moves girls and young women toward the self-regulation they require as adults. Knowledge of the adolescent brain and its important work will deepen self-awareness even further.

CHAPTER 3

Who Am I?
Beginning with the Brain in Mind

> To make a deep physical path,
> we walk again and again.
> To make a deep mental path,
> we must think over and over again
> the kind of thoughts
> we wish to dominate our lives.
>
> —W. A. Peterson

The brain is the source of who we are and what we do. Learning about the brain is step one in deepening your own self-awareness. Developing a working knowledge of changes in the brain during adolescence can make a significant difference in mentoring a girl or young woman. You are role modeling strategies to find your uniquely authentic path through adulthood every step of the way when you accompany a girl or young woman on the journey through her adolescent years. How she makes this journey has a direct impact on how she will live the rest of her life.[1]

At three pounds, mostly water, close to one hundred billion neurons, and more interconnections than there are stars and planets in the Milky Way Galaxy, the brain is the most complex structure in the universe. It should be no surprise that learning about your brain is the best place to start as you seek to deeply know yourself and become more self-aware—and collectively as we strive to support girls and young women to know themselves.

Even more fascinating, we now know our brain is capable of physically changing throughout an entire lifetime and we can directly impact these changes.[2] This exciting recent finding is the reason we begin the GPS for life journey with the brain in mind. Without exception, every single experience we have, whether good or bad, wires, rewires, and changes the physical structure of the brain.

During an experience, your brain cells, called *neurons*, become active or "fire."

Each of your brain's one hundred billion neurons has at least ten thousand connections to other neurons. Every sight, sound, and thought that occurs during an experience activates different circuits in your brain. When neurons fire together, they communicate with each other and grow new connections. Through repeated experiences over time, these connections are strengthened. They "wire together." The networks of neurons form pathways in the brain and become automatic, enabling us to learn, store, and call up information effectively. Think of riding a bike, driving a car, or playing a musical instrument like the piano. Increasing the number and quality of your positive experiences rewires the brain so you can be healthier and happier.[3]

Of course, the opposite is also true. Everything that happens to us—from your family life experiences to those in school and the community where you live to the broader world around you—affects your brain development. If your repeated experiences are negative ones, the networks of neurons or pathways for the negative behavior strengthen. Think of a girl who has a number of bad experiences, possibly including unhealthy or questionable behavior, in social situations. She will eventually view all social situations through the lens of this type of behavior. What does this mean for natural mentoring? It means you, a caring adult, can make a difference.

You can buffer negative experiences by your physical presence: listening, role modeling, and helping girls and young women reframe them. In a similar manner, your supportive encouragement and engagement with positive experiences will shape their brains. Impact their very lives. (Take a breath here. While your encouragement and involved support are impacting their lives, the experiences you share are shaping your own brain in positive ways as well: a residual benefit!)

This was reinforced for me as I listened to separate firsthand accounts of the extraordinary power of a positive lived experience.

Anna and Betsy: Positive Lived Experiences

Anna, seventeen and a high school senior at the time of our conversation, spoke enthusiastically about experiences with Betsy, her teacher and natural mentor. Betsy is a "spark plug" type of teacher who convinced school administrators and parents that student engagement in Model UN activities was a good investment for the Montessori school where she taught. Betsy introduced Anna to Montessori Model UN, an opportunity for students to learn about member countries and make a difference through research and problem-solving. By the time Anna reached high school, she was part of a group of Model UN students who conducted research on the Polynesian island of Tuvalu. They studied challenges and problems the island was encountering. Their research culminated in a presentation at a Model UN convention. Here are Anna's words:

> *Betsy arranged for us to meet with the Tuvalu ambassador and he took time out . . . to sit with all of us for an hour. He asked us questions about Tuvalu and about the issues we were researching about Tuvalu; he knew everything. He just really listened and*

was really interested to hear what we had to say, and he admired our perspective and our feelings about this country that we had grown attached to. He gave us shell necklaces from Tuvalu. That's something like no one ever experiences in their life, let alone when they're a kid. This was an important adult person who really listened to us. It was a very empowering experience.

When I asked Anna about the impact of this type of experience on her, she turned the conversation back to Betsy.

I think Betsy knows the kind of impact that she's had on me and she's seen it through all the work that I do. Her profession and her teaching matters. Also, I'm kind of the one person . . . that has really, really continued on the nonprofit, social justice route. That's been my entire direction in life, so I think Betsy, just seeing me do what I do and knowing that she was the person who inspired that, could help her continue the work that she's doing and know that it matters and it's important.

Some Brain Basics

Anna's experience awakened her to new ways of directing her attention. It physically changed her brain. Until recent breakthroughs in brain or *neuro* science were made possible by brain imaging scanning technology like the fMRI, scientists could study only a dead brain. Today's new technologies can record visual images of live brain activity as it occurs in real time. The ability to "see" inside a brain as it processes information offers new research possibilities every day.

Daniel Siegel, MD, is a pioneer in a new and multidisciplinary field called interpersonal neurobiology. The field seeks common knowledge and practical applications of worldwide research that brings together areas of science such as anthropology, biology, linguistics, mathematics, physics, and psychology. The purpose of interpersonal neurobiology is to promote compassion, kindness, resilience and well-being in our lives through common findings about the human experience.[4]

The field looks at how our brain and our relationships interact with our thoughts and feelings, which are activities of the mind. Dr. Siegel defines the mind as the system that regulates the energy and information flow that come to us continuously during experiences and through our relationships with others. When we view energy as movement from possibility to actuality, this means *our relationships shape our very selves—who we are and who we become.* We can think of this interaction as a "triangle of well-being."[5]

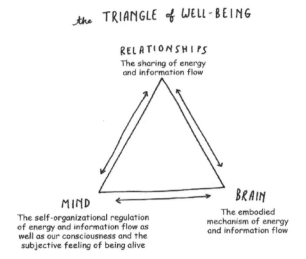

the TRIANGLE of WELL-BEING

RELATIONSHIPS
The sharing of energy
and information flow

MIND
The self-organizational regulation
of energy and information flow as
well as our consciousness and the
subjective feeling of being alive

BRAIN
The embodied
mechanism of energy
and information flow

(Illustration by Merrilee Liddiard as depicted in Siegel, D. J. and Payne Bryson, T. (2018). *The Yes Brain: How to Cultivate Courage, Curiosity and Resilience in Your Child.* New York, NY: Bantam Books. ©2018 Mind Your Brain, Inc.)

The brain is embodied. That means it lives within your body. Think of it as a physical processor for the energy and information that flows from and is shared through our relationships with each other. But the brain is not the mind. Our mind consists of mental activity—cognitive thoughts, language, memory, and emotional feelings—that help us make sense of this energy and information flow. The mind operates as a regulation system that keeps the physical parts of the brain working together in harmony.

We are wired to be whole. When the regions of the brain work together in balance, the brain is integrated. We are "whole brained." We are mentally healthy. We can thrive.

There are two ways for the regions of your brain to be integrated: horizontally and vertically. In the picture below, you can see an overhead view of the brain with the forehead at the top. The brain's halves—its hemispheres—are connected by the *corpus collosum*, a bundle of fibers that runs down the center.

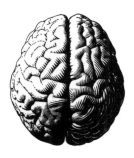

When your brain is *horizontally integrated*, the two hemispheres communicate with each other and work together in harmony. This communication is conducted across the fibers of the corpus collosum. The better the communication, the stronger the fibers become and the more the brain halves work together to support one another as a balanced whole.

Each half of the brain has its own specialized and distinct functions. The left side controls the right side of the body. Its functions are more mental or *cognitive*: logical, sequential, ordered, numerical, analytical, scientific, and linguistic. The right side controls the left side of the body. Its functions are more holistic and creative: nonverbal, artistic, intuitive, imaginative, insightful, musical, and emotional.

Science refers to these brain functions as left- and right-hemisphere modalities.[6] You may have heard a person say they are "left brained" or "right brained." For years, this thinking has been reinforced by "brain assessments" that people can complete to learn their thinking preferences.[7] Science emphasizes the brain works as a whole and integrated system. Nobody is completely left or right brained because each side of the brain reinforces the other. The specialized functions on either side of the brain, working together as an integrated whole, allow us to achieve complex goals that require creative, innovative, and high-level thinking and are the true hallmarks of human capabilities.

When the two sides of our brain are not integrated, we may process our experiences from a purely emotional perspective (from the right side) or a purely logical and analytical one (from the left). We require both: the emotional function of the right side that shows up as emotional feelings and intuition coupled with the logical function of the left side that brings order and structure to all of our life experiences.[8]

Relationships help us make sense of the energy and information that flow from our experiences. Your brain is intensely connected and responsive to other brains starting at babyhood. In fact, a girl's relationships with adults in her life are the most important influences on her brain development.[9] From birth on, the brain and mind develop and mature with the help of all the relationships you have along the way (with parents, caretakers, relatives, friends, teachers, and others, including natural mentors).

Kerry and Judy: Integrating Both Sides of the Brain

When I spoke with Kerry, her rendition of a "highlight" in her natural mentoring experiences with her older stepsister Judy was spot-on as an example of horizontal integration in action. Notice the emotional aspects of the experience, coupled with the logical and analytical requirements of making an important decision. Notice, too, how Judy's calm support assisted Kerry's decision-making.

Kerry was a junior in college facing a life decision. The double major she had chosen in political science and English was forcing her to limit the number of English classes she could take, and she was passionate about writing. She had investigated other schools and was considering transferring, an action that would add an extra year of classes before she could attain her degree. She was emotionally distraught about disappointing her parents. There were many telephone conversations with Judy, and then Kerry came home on a break.

I was a junior in college, and I wanted to transfer, so obviously in terms of numbers, that doesn't make sense for a lot of people. I remember going to her [Judy's] kitchen. She said plainly, 'This is it. This is the choice you have to make. If you do it, that's awesome, and if you don't, then you have to find a way to be okay with it.'

The problem for me was I had finished essentially the part of my English degree and I was furious that I couldn't spend my tuition on more English classes. It was kind of crazy the way it was set up. It was like, even if I drop my poli sci major, I'd already done all the classes that I could, so I was also realizing: Right. Writing is my passion, and if this goes away, then there's no reason for me to be at school. And there's this domino effect of realizing where I wanted to put my money and where I wanted to put my passion . . .

Tons of things were going on. Like, what should I do with my career? What should I do with my education? What do I do with my money? And what do I tell Mom and Dad?

So, in terms of our mentor relationship, definitely the first thing that always stands out to me is this conversation we had [in Judy's kitchen]. That is kind of the moment I decided to transfer. I had this moment of, okay, Judy is here with me. Everything's okay. No matter what I decide, it's fine.

That's kind of a big point in our relationship and in my life. Deciding that was one of the more difficult decisions I've made.

Then I transferred and got my degree in poetry.

Our human connections shape our neural connections. It was necessary for Kerry to use the right side of her brain to see the big picture and use her intuition to envision how she would use a degree. It was necessary for her to use the left side of her brain to think logically about the bottom line of her decision: What was this extra year going to cost? Judy's presence was supportive yet not directive. Through her caring presence, Judy helped Kerry realize for herself she had the power to decide.

Your sense of self is also shaped by your connections to others. People in the lives of children literally shape their brains and help them grow. (This makes the importance of mentoring even more meaningful, right?) As a natural mentor, you are part of the network of caring adults in a girl or young woman's life. Through supportive, face-to-face engagement, your close relationship with her demonstrates love and commitment and that you accept and acknowledge her just the way she is.

Anna's story examined how positive experiences shape the brain. Kerry's story illustrated how a natural mentor can contribute to a young woman's horizontal brain integration. Ellen's story illustrates the power of relationship in shaping the brain to create a unique self.

Ellen: Relationships Help Brain Integration

Ellen's mother passed away when she was eighteen. The sixth of seven children, her three sisters—six, eleven, and thirteen years older—barely skipped a beat in filling the void when this happened, to the point that adult Ellen says in looking back, *My sisters really insulated me from losing my mom. I felt as long as I had them, I'd be okay. I always had my sisters showing me the ropes.*

The three sisters, natural mentors all, each modeled adult behavior in her own way, and Ellen "tried on" each of their personalities:

I observed everything: makeup, accessories, style; tried on shoes and clothes. . . . I didn't know who I was without my older sibs, especially my sisters. I only knew myself through their eyes. They helped me identify my strengths and gifts as a teen/ young adult. That was critically important. I don't think you know that without someone holding up a mirror and pointing those out. . . . They helped me take a bigger view of friends, boys, school. Perspective. I loved that, always relied on it.

The presence and support Ellen received from her sisters, particularly the one closest to her in age, gave her the self-awareness she needed to begin making solid decisions about her life and career.

By the time I got older, I felt like I needed to create my own space for what I was going to do. I never wanted to be compared to them, so I did things that they never did. There were a lot of things I felt like I had ability in or they told me [I did]. If they told me I could do something, I believed I could do it. If they did something, I thought I could do it, but I felt like the challenge would be better to do something they hadn't done. Anyway, that's why I thought it would be great if I went into graphic design because nobody had done that yet.

Ellen's story shows the influence of the brain on our minds and our relationships. Knowing about the brain can help us make sense of our inner experience as well as our social connections to others.[10]

Brain Basics: A Deeper Dive

Understanding a few details about essential brain functions can be a great starting point to self-awareness. Some brain familiarity will help you begin to learn ways to direct your attention so the regions of the brain integrate or work together in a more balanced way. This is essential learning for both adults and adolescents. There are significant differences in adult and adolescent brain architecture. It is helpful to know what is going on inside the adolescent brain, particularly since the period of adolescence is long, beginning around age twelve and continuing to the midtwenties.

Although 95 percent of the human brain has fully developed by age six, we now know that *the second biggest brain growth spurt after infancy happens around age twelve*—at the beginning of adolescence.[11] This is when the brain begins to specialize and "prune" or remodel. The brain literally erases unnecessary or unused connections, making room for new connections and for further strengthening often-used, well-practiced and developed areas. That is why one or two years of piano lessons might not be enough for a person to be able to play the piano years later. With passion, focused attention, and practice over extended time, the brain's piano playing pathway can be refined— possibly to concert pianist level.

Learning new things, developing positive relationships, engaging in sports, and practicing skills creatively through art and music are all positive experiences that encourage the brain to strengthen connections. Gabby and Linda's mentoring story illustrates the power of learning new things and developing positive relationships.

Gabby and Linda: Strengthening Connections through Positive Experiences

When Gabby, the single mother of an eighteen-year-old boy, realized that his girlfriend, Linda was a VIP (very important person) in her son Allen's life, she made an effort to help Linda feel welcome in their home. As time passed, Gabby's interest in Linda's well-being grew stronger and their relationship deepened. Gabby became Linda's natural mentor, drawing her out and helping her express her usually hidden personality. When I asked Linda whether she felt Gabby had anything to do with showing the world her (Linda's) authentic self, I was unprepared for her response.

Okay, yeah, I'll say the dancing thing. It was a while ago. I remember Allen invited me over to have pizza and a [family] dance party. I'm like, 'Dance party? Oh my gosh, I don't know. I don't even know how to tap my foot or anything.' I remember them all dancing and shaking their hips, and they're really into the music, and I'm sitting in the chair the entire time.

The next day, Gabby asked me, 'Why are you so shy? You're such a great person, you have a good personality, why don't you show it?' She didn't say it in a rude way. 'It's okay. You're not going to look silly.' I never realized because my family never danced. When I started hanging out with Allen's family, it was family dinners and games. I was really reserved, and I didn't know how to interact, but I wanted to, and she let me do it at my own pace, and that helped. . . . I think that [dancing experience] was one of the starts of my realizing that it's okay, and you're going to be okay, and you don't have to have rhythm. You're not going to look silly, because everyone else looks silly. I give Gabby all the credit for that. Her voice ringing in my head. I give her all the credit.

On the flip side, detrimental habits and experiences can reinforce and strengthen brain pathways even as those piano connections (after a year or two of discontinued lessons) are being pruned away from lack of use. Unhealthy relationships and tragedies, as well as engaging in questionable social behaviors (drinking, drugs, early sexual experimentation) encourage the brain to strengthen not-so-desirable connections as well.

You may remember Marie, the little girl from chapter 1 whose hair fell out overnight and whose close relationship with her natural mentor, Stephanie, became a source of strength for her. That meaningful life experience prompted adult Marie to seek out a girl to mentor. Since she had no girl who was naturally in her life at the time, she sought the help of her local Big Brothers Big Sisters chapter. Through their matching process, Marie became a Big Sister and mentor to Cassie. They enjoyed a sustained and close relationship (twenty-two years at the time of our interview!) that thrived despite early and ongoing detrimental experiences in Cassie's life.

Marie and Cassie: Reframing through Powerful Positive Relationships

Cassie had experienced a number of personal tragedies by the time she was eleven years old and their mentoring relationship began. Her father was in prison and the family struggled financially. She was extremely close to her mother, who was diagnosed with cancer. After an illness that was excruciating for them both, her mom died when Cassie was sixteen. Cassie was devastated and eventually dropped out of high school.

Marie and Cassie spent time together twice a week for the first four years of their relationship. Marie often included Cassie's younger brother in their outings at Cassie's request. After Marie moved to another city, they continued their connection with phone conversations and emails for the next five years, and Marie drove to spend time with Cassie as often as she could. Their frequent fun and meaningful experiences together uplifted Cassie and boosted her resilience.

Early in their relationship, there were no cell phones, and Cassie scraped together money to call Marie, who commented, *I really think that my drive and desire to maintain a relationship [with Cassie] is a direct result of her drive and her resilience to everything that has gone on in her life.*

Cassie's neural pathways were being wired continually with negative experiences before Marie came into her life. Although the negative home and school experiences did not stop completely, the positive experiences and warm in-person relationship she shared with Marie helped to ameliorate the negative and allowed Cassie to reframe some of her perceptions about life.

Sustained Natural Mentoring: A Critical Success Factor

When we understand the way connections and pruning occur in the brain, the importance of reinforcing worthwhile experiences and discouraging undesirable ones becomes clear. The brain is highly moldable or plastic during adolescence. Here's an important point: *Adolescence is the brain's final period of such intense plasticity.* It is the opportunity of an adolescent's lifetime, and you, her natural mentor, have the capacity to take advantage of this time in a girl's GPS for life journey.

Mentor retention in formal, matched mentoring relationships has been steadily declining in the last decade.[12] Because you are naturally in a girl's life as relatives, teachers, coaches, or adult friends, your sustained relationship with her is a critical success factor in your capacity to positively affect her well-being and help her to thrive.

Together with her parents and other caring adults, your enduring relationship can facilitate her brain's optimal development over time. The significant growth spurt that occurs in the adolescent brain plays out over a much longer period of years than was originally thought. Although science once believed that brain development was complete by the end of childhood, new research confirms the brain matures well into a person's twenties.[13] The timing of brain development and pruning provides answers to some questions about how teens behave. Growing up slowly is prevalent today because it is more common in times and places where people have fewer children and nurture each child longer and with greater intensity.[14]

Brain Physiology: A Brief Brain Exploration

Briefly exploring the regions of the brain can help you visualize where stages of vertical brain development are taking place beginning in childhood through adolescence and into adulthood. As with horizontal integration, the goal of vertical integration is balance and harmony as the vertical regions of the brain work together as a whole.

Before she is born, a baby's brain develops in sequential stages. Different areas of the brain are responsible for their specialized functions. All the brain areas for these functions are present at birth, and as the baby grows, higher functions become possible.

4. The last part of the brain to develop is the outermost layer, the CEREBRAL CORTEX, responsible for thinking, planning, and processing information from each of the five senses. The cerebral cortex takes years to develop and is not fully mature until the midtwenties.

3. The next part of the brain to develop is the LIMBIC SYSTEM, responsible for registering,storing, and processing emotions. The AMYGDALA is part of the limbic system that is responsible for detecting fear and preparing for emergency events. It is programmed to keep us safe. The HIPPOCAMPUS is another part of the limbic system that is responsible for short-term memory.

2. Next, the CEREBELLUM is formed, responsible for balance and muscle coordination. The cerebellum triples in size during a baby's first year, allowing for rapid development of motor skills. New experiences create connections in the brain. Formations of neurons is fastest at birth and slows over time.

1. The BRAIN STEM develops first and is connected to the spinal cord. It relays messages from the brain to the rest of the body. It is responsible for basic survival functions of breathing, swallowing, and heartbeat.

The Adolescent Brain

The Hand Model of the Brain was conceived by Dr. Siegel as a convenient means of communicating with one another about just what is happening in the brain during life experiences. As the graphics below illustrate, the parts of the hand model correspond to regions of the brain. The prefrontal cortex will not be fully developed until the midtwenties, so the adolescent brain relies more on the limbic system and its accompanying emotions to make decisions. Teens are smack in the middle of social, emotional, and cognitive changes, and then bam: puberty enters the picture. Puberty is the start of major limbic changes, particularly because the amygdala's fear detection exercises greater control than the yet-to-be mature prefrontal cortex.

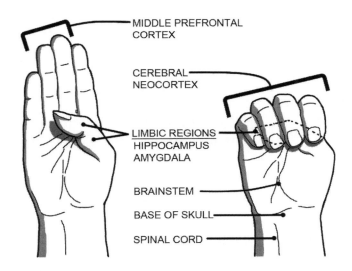

(Dr. Daniel J. Siegel's "Hand Model of the Brain," as first described in Siegel, D. J. (1999) *The developing mind: Toward a neurobiology of interpersonal experience* (1st ed.). New York, NY: Guilford Press. ©1999 Mind Your Brain, Inc., and later depicted by visual image in Siegel, D.J. (2010) *Mindsight: The new science of personal transformation*. New York, NY: Random House. ©Mind Your Brain, Inc.)

This hand model can be a useful and easy-to-access learning prop for visualizing the parts of the brain.[15] If you are explaining to a teen what may be happening in her brain during a life event (such as an emotional meltdown), you always have your hand at the end of your wrist to help you get your points across! By explaining that the limbic system (her thumb) is hijacking her decision-making capability or causing an irrational fear *reaction* of "flipping her lid" (raising all fingers up so the thumb is exposed), she can learn to activate her prefrontal cortex and pause, think rationally, and *respond* to the experience instead (fingers cover the "thumb" limbic system as a representation of more thoughtful consideration in responding instead of reacting).

The *limbic* brain with its component parts is the seat of our emotions. The limbic brain includes the safekeeping *amygdala* and hippocampus, the short-term memory keeper. The limbic brain tells us when we need to fight, freeze, or run away. The limbic brain also remembers. Things that happen to us when we're babies are stored in our long-term memory. During adolescence, the body works with the brain stem as it relays messages from the limbic area to stimulate adolescent emotional growth. Changes in the limbic part of the brain cause an increase in emotional intensity, as well as big differences in what motivates adolescent behavior.

The *amygdala* is the part of the limbic brain that is programmed to keep us safe. It regulates and blocks information from traveling to the prefrontal cortex, so we can react immediately if we need to. We can, however, experience a problem with it. The amygdala can't tell a stressful situation from an actual emergency. *It can cause us to react without thinking.* (Keep in mind, the limbic part of the brain *remembers.* If something traumatic happened to us earlier in life, the amygdala can "hijack" emotions and cause us to react or even overreact to unrelated events in life later on.)

When emotions arise, we use the *cortex,* a part of the brain that developed to help us reason and make sense of what is happening to us. The most recent part of brain development is the *prefrontal cortex,* located just behind your forehead, or the fingers in the brain hand model. This is the main area for self-regulation: planning, making thoughtful decisions, doing calculations, and staying focused on what we're doing.

The prefrontal cortex gets its information only when the amygdala is calm and passes anything it decides is worth remembering to the hippocampus, which stores it in short-term memory. The prefrontal cortex coordinates and balances other regions of the brain but, again, does not fully mature in this process until a person reaches the early twenties.[16]

This is further confirmation that a person's activities and experiences during adolescence are important areas of focus and attention. They stimulate—or stunt—growth in the brain.

The healthy and natural brain changes during adolescence present opportunities as well as risks. The journey to adulthood requires intentional self-awareness and increasing self-regulation. You can encourage the enormous opportunities of the teen years and support girls to avoid and learn to handle the risks.

Adolescents creatively and courageously strive to discover their independent selves. Their voices are just beginning to be spoken yet ready to be heard, encouraged, and celebrated by you. By me. By an adult who cares. The positive characteristics of the teenage mind, if sharpened and refined, are qualities they will carry with them into adulthood. Their creativity and unique thinking can positively impact their communities and the world.

Changes in essential brain circuits cause adolescence to be different from childhood. Dr. Siegel identified four qualities of mind that emerge during brain changes in the early teen years.[17] These are novelty seeking, social engagement, increased emotional intensity, and creative exploration. Each of the changes supports important shifts that happen in thinking, feeling, interacting, and decision-making during the adolescent years. There are upsides and downsides to these changes, with benefits and risks. Natural mentors have an opportunity to maximize the upsides and minimize the downsides of the shifts while supporting girls and young women on their GPS for life experiences.

1. **Novelty seeking** begins in adolescent brain circuitry as an increased desire for rewards to try new things and feel life more fully.

   Downside – Risk-taking overemphasizes the thrill and downplays the risk result. Impulsivity to act without planning ahead or considering consequences can result in dangerous behaviors.

   As a natural mentor – You can first remind your girl that her prefrontal cortex is still developing and will continue to develop through her midtwenties. This helps to explain why she may not plan ahead or consider consequences for her actions. This is not an excuse for her behavior; it is a physical explanation of what is going on. With her parents' or caregivers' permission, you can temper the thrill seeking by cultivating and using organizational skills to help her plan new experiences that will satisfy the desire for novelty.

   Upside – Openness to change and living with passion emerge; the exploration of novelty grows into a sense of adventure for designing new ways of doing things and a general fascination for life.

   As a natural mentor – Depending on your interests and curiosity, the two of you can embrace the desire to live life more fully by planning new and different experiences and projects that you can engage in together on this journey. You can also encourage your girl to engage in this type of planning for herself and her friends, with or without your involvement in the actual experience.

2. **Social engagement** enriches peer connectedness and creates new friendships.

    Downside – Risk-taking behavior increases in peer groups without adult presence. The adolescent tendency to reject adult reasoning increases those risks. Girls and young women are well aware that this time in their life is about preparing for independent adulthood. They are doing their best to head in that direction. They are "practicing" adult behavior, yet their status in the eyes of their peers is uppermost in their minds. Although they may not act like it, they are asking for parental and other adult presence and support in this critical effort. The rejection that "adult you" may experience is not personal! There is a physical and psychological brain development reason behind it. Whew.

    As a natural mentor – You can listen actively and authentically when your girl wants to talk about group risk-taking, resisting the impulse to express shock or disappointment. She needs practice in decision-making when situations are risky. Spending time with her in positive conversation (without cell phones in front of you) sends the message she is worth your time and she can trust you. Teens who report high levels of adult support will engage in less risk-taking behavior because they may be less sensitive to the rewarding effects of risk. They find family and other interpersonal interactions sufficiently rewarding.[18]

    Upside – The social connection drive leads to the development of supportive relationships. These are the best predictors of well-being, longevity, and happiness throughout life.

    As a natural mentor – The supportive relationship you sustain with your girl is a model for her in creating such relationships with her peers. Being present and authentically listening to her when she wants to tell you about her social experiences and relationships, reflecting back what you hear her saying, and resisting the urge to give advice will allow her to be open with you. The greatest gift you can give her is your trust.

3. Increased emotional intensity gives more vitality to life.

Downside – She may be ruled by emotions: impulsivity, moodiness, extreme reactivity.

As a natural mentor – You can introduce your girl to emotional intelligence concepts and help her practice becoming more emotionally intelligent. Returning to the Hand Model of the Brain can help begin the conversation with locating the limbic area, the emotional seat of her reactivity. A simple, effective tool for reducing the intensity of the emotions she is feeling is to name them. This bridges the gap between feeling and thought. There is a six-second window to move out of extreme reactivity and pause, evaluate, and respond in the best way possible.

The most important of these is to slow down and pause. Deep, slow breaths can bring her back to herself. If she needs time to calm down, a walk with a focus on breathing may help. Another strategy to find some space from the situation is to count something tangible, like her fingers, or think of three songs she likes or four trips she would like to take. Three questions can help: What am I feeling? What options do I have? What do I truly want?[19]

Upside – Emotional intensity provides energy and an enthusiasm for being alive.

As a natural mentor – You can share her energy and enthusiasm! Continue to practice the tools of emotional intelligence in all situations. As she becomes familiar with the tools, help her manage her relationships and social situations as a guide to begin to identify her place in the world and possible contributions to it.

4. **Creative exploration** uses new conceptual thinking and abstract reasoning, which opens to questioning the status quo, out-of-the-box thinking, the creation of new ideas, and the emergence of innovation.

Downside – Searching for the meaning of life during adolescence can lead to an identity crisis, a lack of direction and purpose, and susceptibility to peer pressure.

As a natural mentor – You can stay with her as a grounding force and sidekick in this creative exploration. Even adults search for the meaning of life! Share your search with your girl so she knows she is not alone. Together, explore her questions and her thinking. Connect her with colleagues and others with expertise in the fields and areas she finds interesting. Encourage her creativity, her innovation, her out-of-the-box ideas. Take one of them to completion if it's possible. If it's not possible, explore reasons why not. Then take another idea to completion. Help her experience a sense of self-efficacy. Give her hope. We need hopeful teens to be the leaders of the world one day.

Upside – If her mind can continue imagining the world in new ways, when she becomes an adult, she may be able to bypass or minimize the sense of being in a rut that afflicts so many. Instead, she can cultivate the ability to see the extraordinary in her ordinary full life experience.

As a natural mentor – There are many possibilities for you in mentoring your girl as she creatively explores her full life experience. As you live your own full life experience, try on some of these creative possibilities together within this beautiful relationship you seek to deepen with her.

One of the creative possibilities may be learning to be mindful together.

Mindfulness and Mindsight

Mindfulness is noticing your thoughts, feelings, and physical sensations in the present moment, without judgment, in as many moments as possible.[20] It is a valuable way to understand our inner and outer worlds. For young people, it helps build the foundational, key life skill of self-awareness.

A mindfulness practice, also called meditation, is training for the brain. Studies have shown that a mindfulness practice increases areas in the brain responsible for compassion as well as self-awareness. Dr. Siegel's Hand Model of the Brain teaches girls how close the amygdala in the limbic system is to the prefrontal cortex. Mindfulness can help the thinking part of the brain process the raw emotion of the limbic system. That can lead to better decision-making and identity formation during this time when the prefrontal cortex is still maturing. Mindfulness also promotes a mindful pause, leading to an intentional response instead of an unthinking reaction.

You can begin by teaching girls and young women that "mind chatter"—that annoying little voice in your head—happens to everyone. The wandering mind takes them to thoughts of the weekend, to their sports practice after class, to a conversation they had with a friend—and suddenly they spring back to the present, realizing these thoughts have taken them miles away. The frequency of mind chatter increases with the level of stress they are feeling. Today's girls face an epidemic of stress and anxiety. According to periodic American Psychological Association surveys on stress, starting in 2013, adolescents reported feeling more stressed than their parents do.[21] In more recent surveys, their levels of stress have surpassed all other age groups.[22]

To begin teaching mindfulness, start your own practice first. Better yet, start a mindfulness practice together. The breath is an excellent place to start. There are a number of terrific free resources that start with being still, paying attention to your in-breath and your out-breath, and turning inward to "go inside." Among these are the apps Calm, Headspace, and Take a Break! Other resources designed for adolescents are apps called Smiling Mind and Stop, Breathe & Think (SBT).

Consider this as well: mindfulness does not have to be a "formal" practice complete with pillow on the floor and candle burning in front of you. A few of the brief yet meaningful mindfulness habits in the list below have made a real difference in my life. You may recognize a few of them, as versions of them appear in mindfulness-based websites and articles. Try some of the ones in the list that resonate with you and notice the difference they make in your life as well as the life of your girl.[23]

1. Experiment with telling yourself "I get to . . ." instead of "I have to . . ." This can be a mindset changer and often brings in a gratitude perspective. "I get to go to school." "I get to do my homework." "I get to make dinner."

2. Think of your "to do" list as a "to be" list. What am I being as I go about this process of living? Am I being kind? Compassionate? Self-compassionate? Am I being a good friend? A good listener?

3. Stop what you are doing and experience a feeling of gratitude. Take a mindful mental break a few times a day and jot down some things you are grateful for.

4. If you don't have time to write anything down, simply take an intentional pause periodically. Take a minute for a deep breath every hour, after every class, or whenever you find you need one.

5. Do one thing at a time, mindfully. Phone ringing? Take a mindful breath. Having a snack? Notice the look and feel of the food. Savor the smell. Eat slowly, tasting the flavors as you chew. Engage your senses!

6. Practice the pause. When it's time to react, stop. Decide with intention how to respond. Then respond.

7. Keep a gratitude journal. Whether you journal in the morning or at night before bed, every day or once a week, reflecting on what you are grateful for contributes to happiness and a sense of well-being. Gratitude is fuel for the soul.

8. Use the power of a deep breath before you begin a task. Bring yourself to the present moment. Breathe. Mindfully begin.

9. Start your day slowly. Whether it's a cup of coffee or tea, a yoga practice, or simply pausing to stretch before you leap out of bed, savor a few present moments.

10. Practice the intentional pause between tasks. Close your eyes and take a few deep breaths to bring you back into the present. Then plunge in again.

Mindsight is an expanded level of mindfulness. Like mindfulness, it allows us to see the internal workings of our own minds. In addition to being in the now, the present mindful moment, mindsight self-monitors what is happening inside ourselves so we can examine our thoughts, name our emotions, and ultimately modify our behavior. Mindsight is a term that describes our uniquely human ability to closely examine the processes by which we think, feel, and behave. It enables us to link our behavior in the world outside us to our brain's internal or mental processes.

Mindsight is a skill that can be learned and practiced. Through a mindsight practice, you can examine, label, and explain how your internal emotional world responds to the external world around you. Through mindsight, we first focus mindful attention on our inner selves. This enables us to see our whole selves more clearly, to integrate our brain regions, and to enrich our relationships.[24]

When we develop the skills of awareness, focused attention, and intention through a mindsight practice, we change the physical structure of the brain. When it is developed earlier in life, mindsight can become an increasingly valuable means of building emotional strength. When we learn to use mindsight to help the brain integrate the functions of its regions so they work in balance as a whole, we experience the state of well-being.

So how do you start a mindsight practice?

Dr. Siegel has developed a valuable and useful mindsight practice called the Wheel of Awareness.[25] You can begin by picturing your own mind as a wheel with a hub in the center and spokes radiating toward the outer rim. Four segments on the rim represent anything you are aware of or pay attention to: perceptions through your five senses of seeing, hearing, touching, smelling, tasting; bodily sensations from the top of your head to the tips of your toes; mental activities such as thoughts and feelings, dreams and desires, memories and experiences; and perceptions about your connections and relationships with things and people in the world outside your body.

The hub is a metaphor for the inner place of the mind, that knowing place where we are aware of all that happens around and within us. The hub represents our prefrontal cortex that helps to integrate the other parts of the brain. It's from here we make the best decisions. This is the part of the brain that allows us to connect deeply to ourselves and to others.

Our awareness lives in the hub. From here, we can direct the flow of energy and information by focusing attention on various points on

71

the rim of the wheel. We can systematically explore our inner lives by moving around the rim of the wheel. Doing this with focused attention links the elements of our consciousness and helps the brain to become integrated.

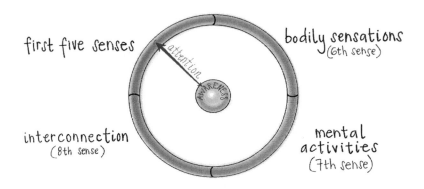

(Illustration by Madaleine W. Siegel as depicted in Siegel, D. J. (2018),
Aware: The Science and Practice of Presence.
New York, NY: TarcherPerigree, ©2018, Mind Your Brain, Inc.)

You can guide the "spoke of attention" from the center, knowing hub of awareness to each segment of the rim of the wheel. Find a comfortable position and try this practice:

1. From your inner hub, focus on your in-breath and out-breath for a minute or two. Then send the spoke of awareness to the first segment of the rim. These are your five senses. Focus on one sense at a time; allow each to fill your awareness. What are you seeing? Hearing? Smelling? Touching? Tasting?

2. Take a slightly deeper breath and move the spoke of awareness to the second segment of the rim. Move your attention to your

body, from the top of your head and scalp, over your face, to the neck and throat, filling your awareness with all the sensations of the muscles and bones as you move down the body, noticing each sensation in the external body. Then focus on the internal organs, moving from the intestines to the stomach, to the interior of the throat, to the lungs, the heart region . . . and finally, allow your awareness to be filled with the interior of the whole body from head to toe.

3. Take an even deeper breath and move the spoke of awareness to the third segment of the rim. Invite into awareness any sensations, images, feelings, and thoughts that may arise. (You may notice this is different from a breath-awareness mindfulness practice that focuses on the breath and lets go of thoughts that distract from the breath.) Here, simply be open to whatever mental life may come into awareness for a few minutes. Then for a few more minutes, notice how these mental images and sensations come into your awareness and are replaced by others. Is there a space between two mental activities in awareness? If so, what does the space feel like?

4. Now find the breath again, in and out. Take a deeper breath and move the spoke of awareness over to the fourth and final segment of the rim. This segment represents our sense of connection to others and to our surrounding environment. Begin with awareness of people close to you in the room, if there are any. Sense their closeness and move on to the sense of connection with your family and friends, then your classmates if you are in school or your work colleagues, to those who live in your community, in your city, in your country, on your continent...to all the people who share planet Earth with you... expanding to the sense of connection you have with all living

beings, animals, and plants. Send compassionate kindness and wishes for health, safety, and well-being to all the beings of the earth and to your own inner self. Find your breath again in and out and take a few final breaths. Gently bring this Wheel of Awareness practice to a close.

Think about the mental activity rim points on the third segment that grabbed your attention. Can you name some?

Possibilities for a natural mentor:
- I'm tired today. I don't know how I can spend quality time with Rosalie (the girl I'm mentoring).
- I'm also irritated that she is late for our time together. I'm going to have to set some boundaries for myself in this relationship.
- I have so much to do when I get home. There's a mountain of laundry in the laundry room.
- I'm worried about her grades. They're slipping and I'm not sure why.
- I'm really tired.

Possibilities for an adolescent girl:
- School was hard today. I hate pop quizzes.
- I want to tell Sue (my natural mentor) about the lunch disaster, but I'm afraid she won't understand.
- I can't keep friends. It makes me so mad.
- I don't understand why the school buses were so late today. Now I'm late for my time with Sue.
- I'm afraid Sue won't understand why I'm late. She's probably thinking I don't care.
- I'm tired.

All these sensations, images, feelings, and thoughts are the rim points on your Wheel of Awareness, and together they determine your state of mind.

What happens when you intentionally direct your attention to other rim points? Slow down for a few seconds, get quiet within yourself, focus on your breath, and ask yourself the questions below.

Possibilities for a natural mentor:
- What's something terrific Rosalie has done that shows me how compassionate she is?
- What's Rosalie's favorite outfit right now? Can I remember how young she looked when we first met?
- I really love being her natural mentor. How would I feel if she weren't in my life?
- Can I picture how she'll look at eighteen, bags packed and ready to leave for college?

Possibilities for an adolescent girl:
- What's something funny my best friend did or said today?
- What's my favorite thing Sue and I have done together?
- Can I picture myself at high school graduation, with my parents and Sue proudly in the audience?
- What's something really cool Sue and I can cook up to surprise my friends with dinner?
- I really like and appreciate Sue. I can tell her anything. How would I feel if she weren't in my life right now?

Feeling different? Has your state of mind changed?

Mindsight was responsible for that. From your hub, you noticed the rim points on your own Wheel of Awareness, and you became aware of what you are experiencing. Then you shifted your focus, directing your attention to other rim points, and as a result, your entire state of mind changed.

This is the power of your mind. This is how it can literally and fundamentally transform the way you feel about and interact with others. Without mindsight, you can get stuck on your rim, feeling mostly frustrated or angry or resentful. By returning to your hub and shifting your focus, you can begin to experience joy and gratitude about being a natural mentor or about being a girl at a growth-filled time in your life.[26]

Mindsight and the Wheel of Awareness help to integrate the many parts of ourselves. When you feel yourself getting stuck on specific points on the rim, remember you can choose where to focus your attention to get control over how you're feeling. You and your girl can practice the Wheel of Awareness together so it becomes more useful and comfortable. Help her pay attention to the sensations, images, feelings, and thoughts within them. Remind each other that feelings are temporary states, not enduring traits. Name these emotions. How can you modify emotions that seem out of control? Help each other think of ways and alternate behaviors to accomplish this.

By introducing the magnificent system that is our brain in this chapter, you can better understand the significance of the role you take on as natural mentor to an adolescent girl. As she progresses along the GPS life journey, she is experiencing a multitude of transitions in the middle of the second most significant brain growth spurt in her lifetime.

As her physical brain does its work in concert with the thoughts and feelings of her mind to make sense of the energy and information that flow through her relationships, she gains the power over a lifetime to reshape its structure. You can help her intentionally orchestrate life experiences and cultivate mindfulness and mindsight practices that help her whole brain to grow and assist her to approach her GPS journey for life in health, happiness and well-being.

CHAPTER 4

Who Am I?

Celebrating Change

> Honor the space between no longer and not yet.
> —Nancy Levin

Change and Transition

"The only person who likes change is a wet baby."

That may be Mark Twain's cringeworthy cliché, but change can feel like a thunderbolt, even when it's desired, carefully planned, and initiated by you. We live in a chaotic world: volatile, uncertain, complex, and ambiguous.[1] Rapidly accelerating, sometimes dizzying change has become the norm in recent years, and it's not going away anytime soon.

Although it can be uncomfortable, even downright painful, navigating change with intention can contribute to personal expansion and growth. In fact, it can reveal another route to follow on the GPS for life!

Consider this back-in-the-day experience from my later teen years:

Off to College: A Personal Transition

I stared out the car window, noticing the trees whizzing by, mostly dark green leaves mottled with end-of-summer color changes. Autumn's transformation was just beginning. I felt oddly connected to this year's seasonal change.

My parents and I were on our way to the University of Illinois, where I would begin my freshman year of college. I was excitedly anticipating the novelty and tantalizingly unfamiliar independence of my next phase of life: a new place to live, new friends to meet, new classes to take.

We pulled up in front of the residence hall. Some students were moved in and purposefully striding toward the bookstore, the student union, the cafeteria. Uncharacteristic shyness gripped me. I kept my eyes on the ground as we unloaded the car. My roommate had not yet arrived, so the empty room filled quickly with my things. First the closet, then the desk. Mom and I made the bed with meticulously selected linens that matched my roommate's. Dad busied himself hanging a curtain rod.

After hiking the enormous campus to visit impressive buildings that housed my classes, Mom put an arm around me as we approached the car. There was a lingering group hug and then they were gone. Completely unprepared for the sudden flood of emotions that swept through me, I raced back to my room. Flinging myself on the bed, I curled up in a ball and sobbed.

It felt like my entire childhood flashed in front of me. How could I leave my dear, wonderful parents, ever the constants in my life? I thought of my younger siblings, probably already reveling in the extra space my move from home provided them. I missed my best-ever high school friends, now scattered across the country having freshman year experiences of their own.

I stayed motionless on the bed for what felt like hours. Then I began talking to myself. "Okay. This isn't productive. Get up. Get out. See who's in the hall. Above all, Stop. Crying!" Then I ventured to the bathroom, washed my face, and looked in the mirror. *What's next?* I wondered.

This experience is but one of the untold number of changes in a lifetime. Some stand out in our memory as pivotal and life changing. As you're reading about one of my standouts, I encourage you to reflect back on one or two of the significant changes in your life.

- What were these standout changes?

- What strategies and behaviors helped you through them?

- Now that you are more self-aware, how might you have navigated these changes differently?

Did I want to begin college? You bet. I wanted to progress from high school to college with everything in me. From the time the acceptance letter arrived, I'd been champing at the bit to leave home. So why was I in tears? What was happening?

It may help to unpack a change event to better understand what is going on inside ourselves. Change happens to everyone, at every age and stage. Knowing some fundamentals of change is not only useful for women, it is most instructive in mentoring girls who move through multiple changes in rapid, bewildering succession and at times simultaneously.

Change is the external situation. I had moved from being a high schooler to a college student, from living at home with my family to living independently in a dormitory. Beneath it all, I was feeling deeply unsettling emotions and beginning to experience the *process of transition.* That meant my world and my place in it felt rocked. In fact, little about my world was the same anymore. It was up to me to find a new path to follow: strategies to intentionally move through the transition so I could internalize and confidently create my new situation, my new relationships, my new life.

Perhaps if my eighteen-year-old self knew about the phases of transition, my working knowledge of the change process may have alerted me to some intentional actions I could take to ease myself through the events as they unfolded. Such practical knowledge is a useful gift natural mentors can give their girls at a young age so the girls can start to navigate their own changes along the GPS for life with attention and intention. Making the effort to transition with intention can help them get to the other side of change on their own terms.

Phases of Transition

What are the parts of the internal transition process? The external change event may be different in every instance and may even be a nonevent—some anticipated change that doesn't occur. For adolescent girls, changes are many and often occur simultaneously. They may include physical, emotional, family, environmental, social, or educational changes. Whatever type of change it may be, the corresponding transition has three phases.[2]

Phase 1 is marked by ending or letting go of the old way and *moving into the transition*. For me, this phase involved a literal move from my family home into an unfamiliar dorm room on a college campus, hours away from where I'd lived for eighteen years.

Phase 2 is the core of the transition process. It is an in-between time during which the old reality is gone but the way forward is yet unknown. It involves *moving through* unfamiliar territory of the change event. This phase requires patience, self-knowledge, and intentional stretching toward a desired result. It can feel frightening to sustain this state of ambiguity and uncomfortable flux. Yet rushing through can affect the quality and the outcomes of change. For me, moving through Phase 2 meant devising a path forward, initially figuring out new processes and a new identity for myself—how to meet people and make friends, find my way around campus, and get to my classes on time.

Phase 3 involves new beginnings, a *moving out* of transition and settling into the change in ways we have carefully and deliberately planned. In this phase, we experience renewed energy, understanding, and a new sense of self, provided we have taken the time to intentionally manage and stretch ourselves as we moved through the transition. New beginnings are marked by different behaviors, new roles, and values that align with the change and give us a sense of purpose. The change is complete.

Although I knew nothing about transition at the beginning of my university life, in hindsight I now understand Phase 2 of the transition process—the stretching, moving through phase—began for me with a decision to get off the bed and out of my room. After washing tears from my face, I walked down the dorm hall to see who was there. An open door to one room revealed four or five girls sitting around talking. I remember standing in the hallway when one of them looked up and hollered a cheerful, welcoming hello! I took a deliberate deep breath and joined them. This was a first step for me in stretching and moving through the transition process. With many more necessary and intentional stretches on the GPS journey ahead toward the goal of becoming an independent college student, my new life as a freshman began.

There was no natural mentor to guide me at the time. When I learned much later in life about the process of intentional transition during change, it struck me that if young girls learned and internalized this critical information, they could put the tools of transition into practice as early as possible in their lives. Natural mentors can role model, guide, and assist them do just that.

Tamara and Jessie: The Impact of Change

When Tamara and Jessie separately told me their mentoring story, I recognized both narratives as classic examples of change and illustrations of the wisdom of intentionally moving through the transition process. Their stories also beautifully highlight the value of natural mentoring to mentor and young girl.

When Jessie was fourteen, her mother ran an international student exchange program in Iran that was headquartered in Washington, DC. The Iranian Revolution was beginning and, although Jessie was one of the youngest exchange students, her mother felt it best to send her to live in the United States. Jessie struggled with depression during her placement with a Rochester, New York, family. To offer her a social environment that included peer and teacher support, she was relocated to a counseling classroom for international students in Washington.

Describing Jessie as *precocious, really intelligent, and really spontaneous,* Tamara, the counseling classroom teacher, began our conversation remembering, *The first thing Jessie did on her first day [in the counseling classroom] was disappear. She got on the subway and went to see the FBI by herself. She went on the tour and then came back as if nothing had happened. I almost had a heart attack.*

Luckily, she spoke perfect English from having gone to the American school in Tehran, but what struck me is she found her way there and she found her way back. I don't know that she had ever been on the subway and she'd never been to Washington, and then she just walked in cool as can be and said, 'Oh, the FBI is really neat!'

I was just stunned. That's when I discovered I could give her anything from crayons to a book to a piece of string and the young woman would just run with it. She had so many talents, music and the arts, and she was a classical pianist and a beautiful artist doing Persian miniatures and she was Just. So. Interesting.

I started learning from her from minute one. She was just brilliant and overly talented, and I say overly because when you're a mentor and you're a teacher, you're pretty straightforward and you stay in your lane so when you get hyper-gifted kids, you feel a real responsibility to them. Then either you start learning from them or you lose them.

I decided I'd start learning from her and collecting her drawings and her stories. She was a great storyteller and she was funny, and I just wanted her in my life. I felt fortunate and excited, and she enriched it so much. Because she was a classical pianist and I played a little bit of piano, I knew something about classical music, but I was really into jazz. When she found that out she was like, 'Oh, okay, I think I'll learn jazz,' and she did. You're kidding me, how do you learn jazz when you're classically trained

*and you're from Iran? She got very interested in jazz and blues.
I had a friend who is a jazz pianist, and we hooked her up with
a jazz teacher. One of her majors is music and I went to listen to
her concerts.*

If Tamara saw extraordinary things in Jessie, the feeling
was mutual.

*When I got to the student exchange and Tamara saw me,
they said, 'This is your teacher.' I felt that she immediately saw a
spark in me, and I in her. She taught me a lot of things, not just
academic. At that time, I wasn't with my parents. She just taught
me how to do things, talk to people, and live. I would call her.
With her, you don't have that thing with your parents where you
want to hide things. With Tamara, I could talk about anything
and I mean anything.*

*A very interesting thing happened. She would make opportu-
nities. She would call my mom and say, 'Can I take your daughter
to the theater?' She kind of became my special friend. I didn't have
a model for that. Over the years, it became a truly reciprocal,
wonderful friendship that was very strong. I think that was probably my biggest mentorship experience, somebody I could look to,
not just for giving me information or attention, but how does she
live? Who can I emulate who's successful? . . . A role model who's
ethical, who cares about me, cares about other people. I learned a
lot from that.*

Jessie's transition from life in Iran with her family to a residential school
in the United States was an enormous change for her. Tamara's introduction to this new student was a change to the composition of her
classroom and a challenge to her as the counselor/teacher. In deciding

to embrace Jessie's quirky, intelligent, interesting self by becoming her natural mentor, Tamara offered a gift Jessie welcomed. She grew to trust and learn from Tamara's interest in her and her ability to role model professional adult behavior.

Intentional Transition: Tools for Resilience

Acquainting young women with change and the transition process helps them understand they're going through many normal changes experienced by all girls on the journey to becoming adults. They are not alone. They're individual persons with common as well as unique change experiences. Whatever types of change they may face, it is comforting to know they are part of the wonderful, marvelous, scary, exciting, bewildering feminine human experience.

The second, stretching phase of transition can be unsettling for everyone, particularly adolescent girls. They have let go of the old ways but may not have a grasp on a desired outcome for themselves, a picture of what the new beginning of change looks like. This phase can be and feel overwhelmingly chaotic. While it may seem best to get it over with, girls need to know that transitions take time and intention. Getting to a new beginning on the other side of change requires soul searching, planning, and vision. How is this accomplished?

There are a variety of tools natural mentors can choose for themselves and introduce to girls to encourage resilience during transition journeys. A toolkit approach that helps girls see transition as an opportunity to learn and grow can be especially helpful when changes seem to be flying at them from all directions. Think back to Jessie. Her experiences demonstrate multiple simultaneous life transitions: a move from Iran to Washington, DC, dealing with the absence of her family, adjusting to a new classroom of peers and a new teacher. During these unique transitions, Jessie was also experiencing the usual adolescent girl transitions of growing up and maturing physically, mentally, and emotionally.

A positive outlook can serve natural mentors and girls well during transition. Planning a process for the transition using a "4S model" strengthens four areas—situation, self, support, and strategies.[3] The model can help women and girls strategize so they feel a sense of organization and are better able to get a grip during change. Natural mentors can role model these areas as they use the model for themselves in the changing times of their own lives. Examining the model with their girls and working through it together, natural mentors can share ways the model may be helping them both on their GPS journeys.

Situation
- What can you do to strengthen your situation? (Think about ways you can seek advice, negotiate, take positive action, and assert yourself.)
- Examine the transition and identify your desired positive outcome.
- What steps can you take to get there?
- Develop an action plan for yourself.

Self
- How do you see yourself? What are your strengths, personality, values? Here is where self-awareness is especially helpful.
- Be kind to yourself. This is called self-compassion. Realize sadness and feelings of loss are completely normal.
- Affirm yourself and your ability to manage change. Think of each transition as an opportunity to strengthen your change management skills.

Support
- Consider what you need during this transition and how you can get it.

- Practice asking for help and support.
- Enlist the help of your family, your natural mentor, other adults.
- Join a group of others facing a similar transition.
- Brainstorm ways to create more support.

Strategies
- What strategies during change have worked for you in the past?
- What new strategies may help you at this time? Think outside the box.
- Again, enlist the help of your natural mentor.

Over time, it helps natural mentors and girls to examine their change management approaches together. As Tamara and Jessie's relationship deepened, they shared each other's journeys. Jessie was a talented pianist; Tamara turned her on to jazz and connected her to jazz musicians. She encouraged Jessie in her art and allowed her the space to grow. Through role modeling her own interests and by connecting Jessie with colleagues and other professionals, Tamara helped her hone her talents and skills and cultivate her strengths. Tamara authored a book and Jessie became a constant presence in each of Tamara's transitions to published authorship.

Tamara often made plans with Jessie so they could have conversations over lunch or dinner about life choices and how to take positive action in one area of life at a time. Creating a transitions timeline is an eye-opening activity for both natural mentor and girl. Looking back at significant life events can be helpful in envisioning a future. Sharing how a natural mentor managed her own transitions, examining both what worked well for her and what did not, are wonderful conversation starters as a girl grapples with managing her current life changes on the journey to adulthood.

Rolling out some butcher paper and drawing a timeline of past, present, and upcoming transitions can be a tangible way to approach the future. Natural mentors and girls can talk about places on the timeline where adult help is requested or required and plan for what that might look like. Scheduling one activity, alone or together—like a daily walk or daily breathing exercises—can have a positive and sustained ripple effect on both natural mentor and girl that can build confidence and resilience.

Building Resilience through Talents, Skills, and Strengths

The National Scientific Council on the Developing Child at Harvard reported the significance of at least one caring adult in the life of a child. Such relationships act as a shield for youngsters against life's inevitable hard knocks, helping them become more resilient. In fact, the title of the 2015 working paper discussing this study is *Supportive Relationships and Active Skill-Building Strengthen the Foundations of Resilience.*[4]

Resilience is the ability to cope with disruptive change and bounce back after change, setbacks, or traumatic life experiences. This set of skills includes maintaining good health and energy under pressure and learning to change to a new way of being when the old way is no longer possible.

Understanding resilience tells us something about how to approach deep and long-lasting natural mentoring relationships. We can open our girls' eyes to their interests, talents, and skills so they can develop them into strengths. We can teach them ways to identify and use resources, such as coping skills and reaching out to trusted adults to nurture their well-being. As their self-knowledge increases, their confidence grows with it. Parents and natural mentors can support our girls in their effort to increase their resilience and experience well-being.

Tamara and Jessie: Honing and Choosing Strengths

Jessie and Tamara's mentoring story illustrates the power of resilience and importance of self-knowledge. In Jessie's case, her talents and strengths were many. The challenge was channeling them into a career. Tamara grappled with her role in helping Jessie to focus. Jessie continued music and jazz through college, graduating with a degree in music. Then she became fascinated with the computer, and because her father is a medical doctor, she considered applying to medical school.

I think for me, helping her develop her strengths was saying, 'You are very gifted. You have all these options, but which ones? Somewhere along the line, you're going to have to focus a little bit.' I think she is still trying to develop that focus in herself. For some people, that's a lifelong process, especially if you're multitalented.

So for me, it was not so much developing her strengths, because she had developed so many even at a young age. It was: Among those strengths, what are the ones that are going to sustain you on a number of levels? She was worried about a job, she worried about her education, and she didn't know what to major in. She was just all over the place in the best possible and most challenging ways. Developing her strengths was more a question of developing her focus on a few of those so she could move forward.

I taught her to achieve her own self-set goals. It was really complex.

Jessie's perspective aligned with Tamara's about identifying and using her strengths.

I think it was her consistency and optimism that gave me resilience. Consistency means that through thick and thin, you're going to make it. It'll be hard, but you'll bounce back and there will be other things. I never felt like I couldn't reach her if I needed her, or once I reached her, she wouldn't be helpful or care.

I'm the type of person who plants a lot of seeds, but I probably don't finish projects as much as I should. It was hard for me to gain a direction. Tamara helped me do that indirectly. My dad was a doctor. It was always assumed [I] would go into the medical field, because that's what [I] knew. That's what [my] parents always talked about. That's what all the books in our house were.

I knew nothing about other kinds of studies and disciplines. At some point, Tamara had worked with labor unions, with workers' rights. She was the head of, I think it was the AFL/CIO branch in Brazil. I started working with labor unions through the recommendations of a friend of hers. Then I started reading things that I was working on. I noticed that every book I'm reading is written by a sociologist. That's when I finally clued in. I was like, 'Oh. This is what I like to do.' Eventually, her inspiration and the things she thought about kind of brought me to what I liked. Sociology has an aspect that is also very quantitative and science-y. I found I could marry them well.

The work I'm doing now with Iranian Americans is perfect. It has a little bit of both. I'm doing a lot of analysis with data sets. At the same time, I'm trying to inspire other young people. This is about civic engagement. It's very exciting.

Identifying and Developing Strengths

Jessie had already-developed strengths at the beginning of her natural mentoring relationship with Tamara. Often a younger girl needs help identifying interests and talents, a first step toward supporting her to develop strengths. Along with knowledge, they are the raw materials of strengths that make us feel energized and alive.

Knowing your own strengths will help young people understand theirs. Positive psychology research studies report that people are happier, more creative, and more productive when using their top or "signature strengths."[5]

The key to building strength is to identify natural talents and then refine them with knowledge and skills.

Here are four clues to help you identify your own talents and help your girl or young woman identify hers:

- *Natural Interests*
  Can you pinpoint instant positive reactions to life situations you encounter? These reactions provide the best trace of your interests and talents because they show where the paths of "least resistance" in your brain are.

- *Desires*
  Pay attention to your strongest, irresistible connections. They exert a magnetic influence. They "call you" and draw you back again and again.

- *Speedy learning*
  Whatever the skill is, if you find you learn it rapidly, your talents may be at work.

- *Enjoyment*
  When you use your strongest synaptic connections, the brain feels good. So if performing an activity feels good, you're most likely using a talent.

Because your special abilities are part of who you are, you may not recognize them as unique strengths. Using your personal strengths seems easy. You may falsely believe anyone can do what you do. Consciously identifying your unique strengths and embracing them as something that makes you distinct helps you to appreciate those special abilities.

Gallup, a global performance-management consulting company, has evidence-based books and assessments to help young people and adults identify their signature strengths. These books and assessments are listed in the Notes section at the end of this book.

Once you both identify several signature strengths, you might identify some things to do to further develop them together. The fun is in the sharing and the excitement that comes from seeing each other improve. The more you do together, the more meaningful your conversations about those experiences can be and the deeper your relationship can become.

Character Strengths

You have the ability to develop physical and intellectual interests and talents into strengths. Jessie in the mentoring story above developed her interest in music into a strength and then used that strength to become a jazz pianist. Your interest in and love for animals can be the start of developing a strength in veterinary science. Your love of movement and dance can be the beginning of strengthening your skill as a dancer.

Besides these types of strengths, each of us also has *character strengths*. What exactly is character? It is the combination of qualities in a person that makes them different from others. This combination is more than individual accomplishment or behavior. Character is another way of identifying "who you are inside"—the part of your personality that other people admire, respect, and cherish. It includes a broad family of thoughts, feelings, and behaviors that are recognized and encouraged across cultures for the values they cultivate in people and society.[6]

In the early 2000s, experts in the field of positive psychology—the scientific study of what makes life most worth living, such as positive relationships, experiences, and institutions— began to ask what is best about human beings.

The field's extensive research around the world identified twenty-four character strengths known as the VIA Classification of Character Strengths and Virtues.[7] As a result, we now have a shared language of communicating with one another about our best selves. Every person possesses all twenty-four character strengths in different degrees, which means each person has a unique character profile.

Character strengths are part of our inner core, the building blocks of our identity. They heighten self-awareness, help us manage problems, and fill in gaps in our self-knowledge. We can look to our character strengths to help us expand the positive and balance the negative in our lives.

Noticing and mentioning character strengths that you see in your young woman or girl is called "strengths-spotting." As she becomes familiar with the strengths you spot in her, encourage her to begin to see strengths in others.

Strengths-spotting involves two steps:

1. In conversation or during any observation of someone in person or a character in a book or a movie, label the character strengths you notice.
   - What is the positive quality you are observing in this person?
   - What character strength word best fits what you're seeing?

2. Describe how you see the character strength being expressed.
   - What is the behavior that is linked with the strength?
   - What evidence supports your observation of that strength?

Cultivating your character strengths has been linked with physical, emotional, social, spiritual, and intellectual well-being.[8] People express a range of character strengths and usually express multiple strengths at the same time.

You can discover your personal character strengths profile by taking the scientifically validated VIA Survey. So can the girl you are mentoring. There is a free adult version of the survey as well as one for young people from ages ten to seventeen. Information about character strengths and the VIA Survey are listed in the Notes section at the end of this book.

The twenty-four character strengths are organized as pathways to six overarching virtues. The virtues are wisdom, courage, humanity, justice, temperance, and transcendence.[9]

Wisdom
Creativity
Curiosity
Judgment/Critical Thinking
Love of Learning
Perspective

Courage
Bravery
Perseverance
Honesty
Zest

Humanity
Love
Kindness
Social Intelligence

Justice
Teamwork
Fairness
Leadership

Temperance
Forgiveness
Humility
Prudence
Self-Regulation

Transcendence
Appreciation of Beauty and Excellence
Gratitude
Hope
Humor
Spirituality

Spotting strengths can involve a third step as well. If you notice a character strength in your young woman or girl, or another person you are with, you can ask yourself, "Why does this person's use of this character strength matter to me, to others, or to themselves?" Then you can affirm the value of the strength and let the person know the strength expression matters to you or in some way benefits you or others.

Developing your character strengths and helping your young person develop hers can be accomplished by learning *what* to know about each strength, *why* the strength is valuable, and *how* to ignite the character strength in your life (reflecting, spotting the strength, taking action and using the strength, and finding balance in life situations by neither overusing nor underusing your strengths but expressing your strengths in optimal ways).

When we amplify strengths rather than focus on correcting weaknesses, it is possible to reframe and learn from the negative. This can be especially useful in times of change and transition. During changing times, both you as a natural mentor and your girl or young woman can take advantage of the 4S model of transition by considering your character strengths. In examining the change *situation* that is occurring, you can both focus on *self* in the model, thinking about how each of your signature character strengths can be most effective in helping you intentionally reach the other side of transition.

In your natural mentoring capacity, examine your *supportive* role by considering which of your own signature character strengths can best help your girl or young woman to navigate change. Finally, use the character strengths you see in each other to develop *strategies* to move through the transition process. When you notice character strengths in each other, take time to initiate conversations about their usefulness during life in general and especially during the transition process. Knowing you recognize character strengths in each other as well as ways to use them during times of change can bolster your girl's self-confidence when she realizes what you are seeing in her. It can also increase her capacity to notice and appreciate character strengths in other people and situations.

CHAPTER 5

Who Am I?

Leading from the Inside Out

> Leadership is
> a series of behaviors
> rather than a role for heroes.
> —Margaret Wheatley

Beginning My Leadership Journey

It was eighth grade. Our Catholic school basketball team was winning that year and, amazingly, we'd won our way to a game with Roosevelt, the local public school. The team and the cheerleaders were beyond excited. Then the unthinkable happened. We all realized the big game was to be held the afternoon of a Great Books Club meeting involving four of the five starting team members and four cheerleaders.

Sister Marie Monica let us know in no uncertain terms that we were leaders in the school and it was our responsibility and our obligation to go.

No, not to go to the basketball game.

We were obligated to go to Great Books Club.

We had a private meeting, all eight of us. It was universally decided we'd go to the game. School spirit and pride, you know.

When we got back to our desks the day after the game, we couldn't find them. Our desks had been moved to the coatroom, all the way in the back of the room. We were separated from our classmates. Sister Marie Monica wouldn't even recognize us when we raised our hands in class. We were to stay this way until we apologized and admitted we had come to the wrong, immature conclusion.

I was devastated and conflicted. This went on for two days. Ultimately, I told Sister Marie Monica I was sorry for shirking my responsibility. But I didn't believe it then and I don't believe it now.

Where was the adult who could have helped me through that trauma? I still wonder.

Leading in a VUCA World

Although I didn't recognize it at the time, and despite my struggle to grasp a teacher's view of what it meant to be a leader, the world was simpler when I was in eighth grade. Today we are in a constant state of change and flux. Have you watched the news lately? It's enough to send you to bed with the covers over your head. The wildly chaotic environment around us calls for new conceptions of what it means to be a leader.

Today's adolescents—from girls in middle school to young women at the beginning of their careers—are members of the generation that will change the world. They are digital natives, born with technology at their fingertips. Exactly how they will accomplish their world-changing is an "unknown known."[1] That is, we know today's adolescents will be a collective force in shaping a world in flux, but we have no idea what the new world will look like. Changes under their leadership could benefit our collective future. Or quite the opposite. Since you and I are today's leaders in a variety of capacities, it is our responsibility to nurture young women on their leadership journey. As their natural mentors, we can walk beside them and support them to be the best leaders they can be.

Future-oriented leadership is required in this chaotic world. The current turbulence calls for a new definition of what it means to be a leader. It is perplexing and challenging even for adults to grasp the many new implications for leadership today. At the same time, it is vital that we convey, model, and transmit a working understanding of leadership in all its forms to young people and particularly to our girls. The acronym VUCA—Volatile, Uncertain, Complex, Ambiguous—is a most suitable descriptor of the world we live in. VUCA first emerged in Carlisle, Pennsylvania, at the Army War College, an army training environment that serves as the graduate school for future generals. The VUCA acronym aptly described the state of the world in Afghanistan and Iran, especially after the terrorist events of 9/11 in New York and Washington, DC.[2]

This VUCA world continues even more aggressively today as a new normal.[3] The disruption of volatility, uncertainty, complexity, and ambiguity is not going away anytime soon. Wrapping our minds around the implications of such disruptions may be confusing and frightening, but it is crucial not to stay frightened.

Instead, we must engage with the confusion and the fear using a method to convert or flip fear into opportunity. This is a leadership skill the Institute for the Future calls "dilemma flipping." A dilemma is a situation that has no clear choice or answer, a problem for which there is no known solution. The ultimate challenge in the midst of the VUCA dilemma is to change our perspective of the world—and our girls' perspective—from a threatening thing, which it certainly is, to viewing it as a world full of fresh opportunity.[4]

Let's unpack the meaning of VUCA to get a clearer picture of our changing world so we can effectively lead and prepare our girls for leadership. In cultivating the skills required in a VUCA world, we are readying our leaders of the future to thrive.

V Is for Volatile

In a *volatile* world, things are liable to change suddenly, quickly, and unexpectedly—and often for the worse.[5]

Examples of this volatile world that adults and adolescents can readily grasp are:

- A school shooting
- A flu epidemic
- Climate change
- Terrorist attacks

A volatile world requires the skill of *vision*. When girls are able to see through the chaos, they can guide themselves with increasingly clear self-awareness. As you support a girl on her GPS for life journey, helping her identify her unique strengths and values will begin to clarify her vision of where she is headed and create strategies for how to get there. Your encouraging and consistent presence will be an important factor in boosting her resolve to stay on a course she has set for herself. Your authenticity in listening, responding, and sustaining her feeling of being respected, felt, and truly heard will be key to her success in refusing to let external events and people influence her in negative ways.

U Is for Uncertain

In an *uncertain* world, things are questionable, unsure, not known or definite, not clearly defined, not determined.

Some information may not be available, but the current event—whatever it may be—and its basic cause and effect are known.

Examples that may be meaningful for adults are:

- Two companies merge into one. What jobs will be lost? How do you prepare for an uncertain future?
- You plan to launch your new coaching business then hear your colleague just launched hers. How will you get clients and preserve your relationship?
- You become an engineer because you're an introverted math whiz then learn you must interact with others to share your wonderful ideas.

Examples that may have more meaning for adolescents are:

- The 2020 COVID pandemic forced high schools to pivot to virtual classes. It became necessary for students to take and pass virtual classes for an unknown length of time until in-person classes resume. How can students successfully navigate the uncertainty of online learning? What study habits are required?
- School systems are required to provide increasingly comprehensive security training plans and school crisis response drills and exercises. How will students cope with a potentially frightening array of drill experiences that target physical and psychological safety in vulnerable areas?

An uncertain world requires the skill of *understanding*. With her vision beginning to take form, a girl's deepening understanding of herself and her capabilities allow her to use her strengths to take advantage of rapidly changing circumstances that are the norm, not only in the VUCA world around her but in her everyday adolescent world. In exposing her to a variety of viewpoints and information sources, she will have the benefit of other adult role models and your support as she begins to discern her voice and direction from the many choices in her path.

C Is for Complexity

In a *complex* world, the situation has many different interconnected parts and variables. Some information is available or can be predicted—but the volume or nature of it can be overwhelming to process.

Examples that adults may find meaningful are:

- Your business has grown from local to national to international. Each country has unique cultural values, regulatory environments, taxation. How do you navigate these changes and thrive in your business growth?
- The persistent presence of poverty and inequality is inescapable. Where can we begin to make a difference?

Examples with meaning for both adults and adolescents are:

- You live in the dry southwestern part of the country. Your home—your whole town— has been destroyed by fire. How do you begin to rebuild your life? How do you cope with the emotions that accompany this trauma to your life as you knew it?
- Unemployment continues to rise among younger generations. What steps do we take to begin to change this trend?

A complex world requires the skills of *clarity* and *courage*. As a girl progresses through adolescence, the vision she has for herself becomes clearer as she journeys through the events in her life and makes sense of them within the larger context of her community and a changing world. Her self-awareness deepens steadily. With the increase in self-awareness, she refines her strengths through activities and projects. She actively changes her physical brain structure by practicing skills of interest to her journey. With your support and feedback, she finds the courage to begin to use her newly identified voice. She summons the courage to take necessary risks and make bold moves on her own behalf. Through all of this, you have her back and she knows it.

A Is for Ambiguity

In an *ambiguous* world, causal relationships are completely unclear. No precedents exist; you face "unknown unknowns."

One example adults can relate to may be:

- You decide to move into another marketplace to launch a business or product outside your core skills and competencies. This requires experimentation and scenario planning.

Another example that has meaning for both adults and adolescents is:

- Your spouse's work—or your own work—requires the whole family to move to another country for an indefinite length of time. What are the implications for schools, making friends, cultural norms, living accommodations, security?

An ambiguous world requires the skill of *agility*. For your girl, this means forward momentum and adaptability as she changes and evolves along with the circumstances in her world and the disruptions of the larger world around her. She is on her way to becoming an agile leader: a creative thinker with a deep sense of purpose. Leadership potential grows through learning agility. Agile leaders are agile learners who thrive as they solve difficult problems. Learning agility is her ability to remain open to new ways of thinking and continuously learn new skills. The ability to learn and adapt throughout her lifetime will determine how well she is able to thrive in a VUCA world.[6]

You are your girl's natural mentor and can help her navigate and grow in this world of unknowns by engaging with and supporting her as she strives to reach her highest potential. Although many adolescents find themselves without this type of support, adults who are naturally in their lives—relatives, teachers, coaches, parents' friends—are too often unaware of their own ability to make a difference.

Think back to my story of the basketball game and the Great Books

Club meeting. My own eighth grade teacher could not or would not empathize with my decision-making difficulty in the "to go to the game or not to go" dilemma. If she had taken the time to engage with me, to help me make sense of the situation and my role in it, perhaps we both could have reached a higher understanding of each other's perspective. When a caring adult takes an interest in a girl's world, she demonstrates authentic respect for the girl just as she is. Their relationship grows as she helps her girl learn ways to make unique contributions. Confidence builds. Leadership begins to blossom. A girl's path on the GPS for life becomes clearer.

Ripples of Leadership

To lead others, it is necessary to lead ourselves first. In this sense, we are all leaders. Leadership starts within and progresses outside oneself to leading many. To truly grasp what it means to "lead yourself first," let's zero in on a useful three-level leadership model for today's world.

The model's three concentric circles move from the center to the rim. Personal or self-leadership is surrounded by private leadership, defined as the influence of one person to another. These two are encircled by public leadership, defined as the influence of one person to many.[7]

THE THREE LEVELS OF LEADERSHIP MODEL

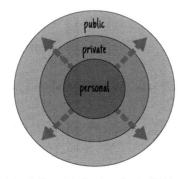

(Adapted with permission from James Scouller, 2016.)

Of the three levels, personal leadership in the center of the model is the most powerful to develop. Personal leadership grows like ripples that spread out from the center when a pebble is tossed into a pond. At its core is your own *self-awareness*, which you acquire in progressive stages as you learn to lead yourself first.

Inside-Out Levels of Leadership

As highlighted in chapter 2, self-awareness is the cornerstone of emotional intelligence. It opens to self-regulation and your growing connection with others. The strengths you identify and develop into knowledge and skills become your "technical competence."[8] Taken together, your deep self-awareness, the quality of your relationships, and your technical competence are the building blocks of self-mastery. Personal leadership is the inner heart—the source—of your potential outward leadership effectiveness.[9]

The chapters in this book are written to help you walk with a girl as she develops personal leadership along her GPS for life journey. Opening up and acquainting her with your own "whole self" is one step in establishing trust between you. That trust goes a long way to nurturing her comfort level with you as she begins learning about her own whole self and gradually discovering who she is.

Sharing what you've learned from Chapter 3 about physical characteristics of the brain, and the exciting changes happening in hers during adolescence, provide food for conversation, speculation, and future foresight as she navigates life during this time. Her self-awareness will further deepen as you navigate and celebrate the many changes taking place in both your lives, figuring out together some ways to intentionally transition toward desired outcomes along the journey.

Private leadership, the second level in this model, refers to individual one-to-one handling of relationships. This includes getting to know people as unique individuals, agreeing on individual goals to support the connection, helping and supporting people to grow. These are the same ways we nurture a natural mentoring relationship, peer friendships, or relationships in an organization like school or a business.

The outermost level of the model is public leadership, the actions a leader takes in a group setting. This is "togetherness building"—encouraging group-wide trust and respect and developing an atmosphere in which it is desirable to perform to a high standard, to share information, and to help others.

Illustrating Inside Out Leadership

Girls can begin to grasp the "leadership from the inside out" model at a young age. It can begin with simple role modeling. Addie's story about her experiences with April in three years of first being her nanny, then realizing she had become a natural mentor to April illustrates how a college student can influence the *personal leadership capacity* of a ten- to thirteen-year-old.

April's friends—and I think just that age group in general—kind of like to pick on each other and pick things they don't like or that they don't agree with and maybe not speak highly of everyone. I made her think a lot more about how her words can affect someone. I've noticed a huge change in her from the time she was ten and now [age thirteen at the time of our interview]. She used to go along with her friends in picking on people or gossiping about other girls in her class, and I would just say little things like, 'Well, I'm sure that's not true about her,' or 'I'm sure you don't know the whole story.' Now I find April saying the same kind of things to her friends when they start talking about that kind of stuff, which is just really cool to see that.

April learned about improving the quality of her relationships through her conversations with Addie. She grew in self-awareness through her natural mentor's comments and questions, moving toward self-regulation and, in the process, deepening her connections to others. With Addie's help, April was learning to develop personal leadership, the center and most powerful part of the leadership model.

And the learning goes both ways! Many of the women who spoke with me talked about their own deep learning through the experience of natural mentoring. Thinking ahead to her own leadership as a future teacher, Addie expressed gratitude for her time with April:

I think especially as a future high school teacher . . . when I got to college and started taking classes on adolescent development, I was like, 'Wow, April is going through this exact same thing.' I'm so thankful for having an example and really just a friend and a sister that could teach me about all of these things that I'm learning about in my textbook but also show me the struggles of being a young tween and teenage girl—and that that's actually a hard place to be. I'm going to have girls in my class eventually in less than two years that are going through the same thing. April has shown me what the best ways to deal with those situations are, and how not to get frustrated all the time, and practice patience and humility and love and understanding that it's a hard place to be and that deserves to be respected.

Addie's involvement did not just contribute to April's personal leadership. Role-modeling opportunities and one-to-one conversations with April also strengthened Addie's second level, one-to-one private leadership.

Their interactions led to better strategies for Addie in coming up with questions that would open April's eyes to herself during situations with her friends. Natural mentor Addie benefited from engaging in those conversations that resulted in learning for both of them.

The knowledge that to lead others we must lead ourselves first is part of self-awareness. Our sense of well-being and ability to self-regulate depend on the harmonious way our brain regions integrate or work together as a whole. An integrated brain processes the information and energy flow we share in relationship with others to create the "self" we perceive ourselves to be as well as the "Self" with a capital S, the highest form of our future selves that we envision. So relationships are not just connections between and among people. We are who we are, and our sense of self exists *because of* our relationships. Addie's natural mentoring story demonstrates how over time, April's sense of a 'kind self' matured and grew through her interactions with Addie.

The inside-out model of leadership makes sense to girls. They learn to see themselves at the heart of the model. Understanding that leadership begins internally with leading yourself, and grows externally through relationships with others, aligns with what we know about the brain.

There is a growing body of research suggesting that what is happening in our brains can improve our leadership skills. NeuroLeadership merges two fields, the study of the brain—neuroscience—and the field of leadership. It is intended to help individuals and organizations of all types reach their potential through better understanding how the human brain functions at individual, group, and system levels. The field is grounded in the brain science of four leadership activities: how leaders make decisions and solve problems, how they regulate their emotions, how they collaborate with others, and how they navigate and facilitate change.[10]

These four domains provide a foundation for both research and education. The changing VUCA world of today requires the type of leadership that originates with self-regulation and progresses through the hard work and resiliency of a growth mindset. NeuroLeadership studies how the brain affects public leadership, the third level in the leadership model, and the brain's impact on individuals within organizations. As a natural mentor, your understanding of NeuroLeadership can help you acquaint your girl with its work as she learns about the connection between her own brain and leadership.

System Leadership

An expanded view of leadership grounds women and girls as members of the broader global community. This view extends beyond the one-to-many concept of public leadership in the inside-outside leadership model. For that reason, the adapted model below reflects a fourth circle at the rim: system leadership.

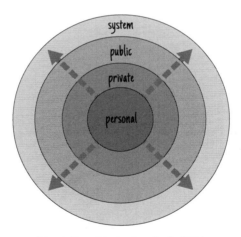

(Adapted with permission from James Scouller, 2016.)

Grasping that leadership grows from inside the individual and extends beyond public leadership to the systems in our world is another critical skill for a VUCA world. The planet faces systemic challenges beyond the reach of our existing institutions. Volatile, uncertain, complex, and ambiguous dilemmas and problems like many we identified earlier in this chapter (climate change, rising unemployment among younger generations, poverty, and inequality) are serious issues that require us to collaborate and work together—crossing individual, organizational, and international boundaries,

They also require a unique type of public leader who is able to draw on and bring about *collective or shared leadership*. She is a system leader, possessing qualities that enable her to achieve seemingly impossible changes by tapping the combined intelligence, spirit, and energy of many people.[11]

There are three core capabilities of a system leader:

- She sees the larger system rather than just its parts.
- She fosters reflection through mindsight and shared, open conversation.
- She shifts focus from reactive problem solving to co-creating the future.

Public education is an example of a system of interconnected parts. One classroom of students is connected to a school of classrooms, which is connected to a district of schools, connected to the statewide and then the national educational system. Educators have selected a career that links them to young people on a regular basis. Each educator is in a perfectly designed space to role model, support, and mentor not only students but each other.

We'll first look at educators as leaders and natural mentors of other educators.

Leaders in school districts have long recognized the value of mentoring new staff members. Many districts have formal mentoring programs in place that pair experienced teachers with newcomers.

It is fascinating, however, that successful, long-lasting mentor pairs often come together organically. They initially "see" something in each other, seek each other out, and intentionally invest time in each other.

Judith, an elementary school leader and principal in Columbus, Ohio, commented about this during her interview with me:

You said something I see so much in my line of work which is the 'natural mentor' as opposed to the assigned mentor. I work in a state where it's required that I as the principal pair a new hire or a new teacher. The [experienced] person earns a little bit of money to be the mentor and I always tell the new teachers this: 'Your real mentors are going to be the ones that come out of the woodwork. The ones who relate to you personally, the ones that are understanding your journey because it's also their journey. The ones that see something in you that they want to foster. And those will be the mentors that I'm not assigning.'

[These relationships] will just happen naturally, and it's really fascinating to watch how it happens. Similar personality, similar background, desire to help, whatever it is. Those are the ones that turn out to be the rich mentoring relationships.

Christine, Judith, and Valerie are three generations of educators whose relationships embody natural mentoring. Judith said:

I do have a strong feeling about mentoring because I have been so lucky along the way. At times, I really needed a mentor and the right one came at the right time. I'm an elementary school principal. Once I got into teaching, I was so lucky to have Christine, a principal who believed in me much more than I believed in myself at the time. She said early on, 'You're a leader. You're going to be a leader someday.'

I didn't even really know what that meant at the time, but she just asked the right questions. She was one of the most magnificent mentors I had, a woman who really laid a path for me as a professional. In her day-to-day work, I saw someone who was incredible in making a big difference in the world. I aspired to be like that.

Christine hired me as a teacher. She had a kind of aura about her where people just wanted to do things for her. . . . People wanted her admiration and respect and attention, and I really studied that. I thought, What is she doing to make that happen? *Because she would say to a group of staff members, 'Okay, we need to jump now,' and they'd all jump.*

I watched, and I listened. I learned, and I decided I'm not just going to be a teacher. . . . She let me stumble. She let me fail. I think of her a hundred times a day because I'll think of a way she handled situations and why. I think of the fact that I'm doing this work I passionately believe in, and I think it's exactly right for me, and she saw it before I did. She was my principal for seven years, and then I worked as her assistant principal for three. Then she retired and we stayed very close in touch. Even after she retired, she'd have us over to her home for dinner. We probably have lunch two or three times a year.

And none of that was about control or power with her, ever. To this day when she looks at me in the eye, she'll say, 'I'm so happy for you,' and she means it. That's very rare with women, which is sad to say, but for a woman to genuinely celebrate and be happy for another woman's success when they're not part of it is a rare thing. I've learned that the saying 'Women don't compete; they empower.'—that's what it should be. We should all be wishing everyone wins, and I think that was the biggest lesson that she taught me.

From Christine's perspective, generational differences colored her initial conception of mentoring.

"I would say my experience was lack of mentoring. There was no one around me that could serve as a mentor or a model or tell me what I needed to do or how I should do it or what was important. I had one other middle school principal who was very helpful, but as you know, there are differences in the way women approach things and the way men approach things. What I was finding is, if I wanted to follow anyone . . . I would have to interpret what they did versus my woman's intuition. So it was a matter of, 'Okay, this is the way a man would do it. Now how would a woman do it?'

Then during the late '90s and early 2000s, women were starting to be recognized as having unique qualities for leadership, which was a good thing for me and other women, that women could bring their own special talents and abilities to leadership positions.

And in fact, women were more intuitive, understanding. When I started, it was like you had to be very tough. The only thing I knew was if I was going to compete with the men, I had to be tough. It was very different then. From that, I decided, 'Okay. Now I need to help other young women recognize their unique talents and their abilities and how they approach the work.'

What I found was I was happy because I was really good at it. I was able to be tough, but I could be very hardworking, very intuitive. . . . . I discovered for myself what I was good at, what I needed work in, and I felt good about what I brought to the profession in terms of leadership from a woman.

Christine saw leadership in Judith, one of the three generations of educators mentioned earlier, from the time she hired her as a teacher. She knew Judith was a leader before Judith knew it herself.

As a building principal, I had at one time a staff of over one hundred people. I had a large middle school, eleven hundred students, one hundred staff members. I was always, I think, in a position of mentoring my teachers, and I hired Judith as a teacher.

As a woman, I was able to clearly see abilities and what I needed in what position. Teachers can be very stability-seeking people, and sometimes it's hard for them to take a risk. I hired Judith as a new hire from out of town. Immediately I saw in her the heart to do the work. It's not only skill and talent. It's not only hard work. It's whether a person has in them what they need to do the job. It's a very internal ability to see and do things, show a lot of initiative, begin anew, and do all these things that I guess require not only skill and talent and smarts but heart to do the work.

That's what I saw in Judith. I just saw this innate ability that she had that I needed to tap because she just had it. I could see in her not only the seeking to do the job well and learn the job— because she didn't have all the skills at the beginning. I hired her as a teacher first and then as an assistant principal. We worked together in both the teacher and assistant principal relationship, and then she went into administration. She really learned quickly. You can just see that in someone. The first thing I did was help her become a team leader, and she started working on some projects that showed her leadership.

During my interviews with women on both sides of the natural mentoring table, I often learned those who had been mentored had gone on to mentor others later in life. Christine mentored Judith, who in turn began a natural mentoring relationship with Valerie when she and Christine hired Valerie as a new teacher in their school district. Here is an excerpt from Valerie's mentoring story:

Christine and Judith interviewed me, and I think I'd just graduated college. I was twenty-one at the time, and I just instantly remember connecting with both of them. . . . I knew instantly that was where I wanted to work, and they offered me the position. Very quickly Judith and I connected. It's funny. You talk about emotional nurturing, and I remember where her office was—and she had peanut M&Ms in her office and I would just go in and shut the door and just talk to her about relationships and my struggles.

Christine was only there with me for one year, but I met with her after she left. She would take me out to dinner and just talk with me about being a woman in this field. She was really a pioneer with that good ol' boys kind of club. She stood up to them, and she was strong. I think that resonated with Judith, who was one of our lead principals there and has written books and is just incredibly strong and a real trailblazer in our professional world.

There was an assistant principal position at her building that came available and of course I was like, 'Oh my gosh, I would have a chance to work with Judith. What a great person for me to learn and grow from. We have this great relationship. I think we would be a great team.'

She was so professional about it. We never talked about it before the actual interviews. They were very formal, and she followed the process. It wasn't like I had a leg up on anybody. . . . I ended up not getting the position, and it devastated me. I shut down.

> *A week later she sent me an awesome email: 'Hey, I know you are upset, and you are going to take the high road. You're never going to let anyone see you are upset.' It was all the right advice at the right time. It took me a long time in that grieving process, and I felt wounded from it and hurt. Her answers to me were the right ones and it's the [leadership] reputation I wanted to have all along.*

Girls whose journey to adulthood includes a deep relationship and meaningful experiences with adults who amplify their self-awareness can grow into leaders with the necessary capacity to turn vision into reality. The reason? These girls and young women are starting the journey at the center, with personal leadership. They are learning to lead themselves first. At the same time, they are learning to master the next level, one-to-one leadership with each other and the significant adults in their life.

As natural mentors, adult women have the privilege of being those significant adults.

True leadership
stems from individuality
that is honestly
and sometimes imperfectly expressed.
Leaders should strive
for authenticity over perfection.
—Sheryl Sandberg

CHAPTER **6**

Who Am I?

Finding and Using My Voice

Today you are You,
That is truer than true.
There is no one alive
Who is Youer than You!
—Dr. Seuss

What does it mean to "be you"? Aren't you always "you"? Is there ever a time when you're not? Does the "you" inside match the "you" the world sees? Makes you think, doesn't it?

When a baby is born, she knows nothing about who she is. She is simply, beautifully, purely herself. Over time, she learns there are important people around her who will feed her, keep her warm, change her, bathe her. She learns how to get their attention. She cries! Loudly.

Gradually she learns to focus on these people, usually her parents or caretakers. They hold her close, love her. They smile. She smiles back and realizes this small response delights them. When they tickle

119

her, she laughs. They are enthralled! She is learning how to "be" in her world. She quickly figures out how to perform so she gets what she needs and wants.

This behavior continues as she grows and begins to explore the outside world around her. She is still operating from her tender inner self, the only self she knows, and her way of being expands with the number of individuals in her life. She learns different people and situations require distinct ways of being. As she makes friends and interacts with peers more and more frequently, she observes. She discovers certain ways of presenting herself that work well with some friends but not others. She adjusts accordingly.

With the beginning of school, she faces the expectations of her teachers. Through trial and error, she revises aspects of herself to meet these expectations as she perceives them. She may hide parts of her tender inner self to fit into this new, confusing environment. She may even build an imaginary wall of protection to keep herself safe. Inside the wall is her "true" self. Outside the wall is her "social" self.

She continues to observe, to learn, and to grow as a social being. As she enters adolescence, her friends become increasingly more important to her. She may "try on" a few personas to fit in with the social group she is with at the time. In fact, she may change herself to match nearly every situation: in school, she may be the "good student." At a party with one group of friends, she may be the "wild girl." At another party with a different group of friends, she may be the "comedian." At home, she may be the "quiet one."

How does she learn to express who she truly is inside? How can we help her feel safe enough to allow that vulnerable inner self—her authentic self—to be seen? What fundamental or core values might guide her behavior and support her in distinguishing between right and wrong?

Core Values

Your beliefs become your thoughts.
Your thoughts become your words.
Your words become your actions.
Your actions become your habits.
Your habits become your values.
Your values become your destiny.
—Mahatma Gandhi

Values are a person's "measuring stick" for what is important to them.
They are principles or standards of behavior and beliefs that make
up the personal components of a good, well-lived life. As children,
we base our thoughts, words, and actions on shared family, spiritual,
ethical, societal, and cultural values. In adolescence, young people
begin to consider personal values that apply uniquely to themselves:
How do my beliefs align with those of my parents? My friends? My
teachers? What values of theirs most clearly embody the life I want to
live? What other values apply to my life? Of these, which two or three
stand out for the way I want to live *my life right now*? These are my
personal core values.

Adults in a young girl's life can strongly influence the development
of her personal core values. Examining your personal values from an
adult perspective from time to time clarifies where you are in your
own life journey. Sharing this values-examination experience with the
girl in your life through conversation is one way to introduce the
importance of assessing your life and identifying values that apply
to your current situation. By doing this, you role model living by
core values.

When an athletic girl identifies "optimal health" as one of her core
values, it colors the way she lives her life, the choices she makes, the
friendships she cultivates. During times of those difficult adolescent

decisions—"Do I accept and drink this beer?"—an optimal health core value can help her muster the courage to refuse. When she arrives at this decision based on her own value of optimal health, she is calling up resources from within herself instead of solely relying on external forces ("Mom and Dad will ground me for the rest of the school year!") to lead her.

Many of my interviews highlighted mentors whose presence deeply influenced the values of the girls in their life. Below are excerpts from three.

Miranda was the first woman who knew I had decided to write this book. When she learned of my plan to interview women who had been mentored, she said, *Oh, you need to talk with me! I had the most wonderful natural mentor ever.*

My values came from my grandmother: honesty, hard working. She was kind, she was spiritual, she was giving. The work ethic and the willingness to go to school and learn to be something were modeled by her and my uncle.

Being a good mom is a strength I got from her. She built my confidence, let me know I was okay, there was nothing wrong with me, that mistakes are okay. Allowing me to make mistakes and then continue allows you to know you can be a leader. She was my authentic 'self-guidance person.' . . .

My grandmother knew all my secrets. She knew all my faults, but she also knew my strengths. She's the one I learned to cook with. I'd be in the kitchen and she was patient and tolerant. I remember putting macaroni in before I boiled the water, and it failed epically.

But it wasn't a big deal, and I think that's part of mentoring—you experiment with things. You experiment, and you can fail, and the world doesn't fall apart.

She gave me that rope to kind of do some things by myself, but she was there for me no matter what. She was a role model in so many ways that you could be selfless and give.

You matter and it's okay. It's okay if you're human. That allowed me to start thinking about me . . . and where I fit in the world. Just that unconditional love made me self-aware in thinking I am okay and I'm valuable in this world and how do I fit in and what can I do for others?

She was part of my life change. After my father passed away, I was looking to try and get back to school. She and my uncle opened up their house to me and I was able to move to Boston and go to school. I was able to live with them and save money. I couldn't have gone to school without her.

Consider again the natural mentoring experience of Anna, the seventeen-year-old high school senior you met in chapter 3, whose mentor of nine years, Betsy, was her teacher in third grade:

Before I met Betsy, I didn't know what was going on. I was a little kid. I thought, oh, everybody had my life. Everybody had food on the table all the time and everyone had parents that loved them. I wasn't aware of sexism that I would face or just prejudice in general. The fact is she deepened my values because she showed me that there was a world outside of these million-dollar homes in Scottsdale and that you should care about people that you don't even know. She taught me how to be a compassionate person. In terms of my values, compassion is really something that she instilled in me and feeling a responsibility for the problems that you see around you.

Valerie, the school administrator you met in chapter 5, spoke enthusiastically about multiple kinds of mentoring. She was one of three
connected women I interviewed—Christine, Judith, and Valerie—who
had been mentored and were mentoring other girls and women in the
school district where they worked. During the interview about Valerie's
experiences with her principal's mentoring, Valerie started the conversation by talking about her grandmother.

> *This has been such a great experience for me in considering
> my relationship to mentoring because it has challenged me to
> think back over all these years. . . . I have had people as mentors
> at different stages in my career, at different points in my life—
> and it's been everybody from my grandmother to friends at work,
> colleagues at work, my family . . . and they each have a specific
> juncture.*
>
> *The story of my gammy is an even more interesting one. She
> is not a biological grandmother, but she has known me since I was
> born. Her biological son was killed in an automobile accident
> right at the time my dad's parents both died of cancer within a
> year. The best way I can describe it is they pseudo-adopted my dad
> as their son and he pseudo-adopted them as his parents when they
> both tragically lost loved ones at the same time.*

My aside: this couple became natural mentors to Valerie's dad and,
in the process, "grandparents" and natural mentors to Valerie.

> *So when I was born, both my natural grandparents had
> passed away. You know those calendars that new moms will write
> every day about what you did? My mom kept a calendar. 'You first
> rolled over.'. . . "Today you said your first word.'. . . 'This is what*

we did today at the park.' Well, almost every single day I was with my grandma, my gammy. I have always known her as such.

When my grandpa retired, they moved to North Carolina. We kept in touch, and then they relocated to the Columbus area, which is where I live now. I reconnected with her after I moved to Columbus when I graduated from college and got to know her in a way that was different from me being a part of my family. It was just me as Valerie, a very different way.

I lived in my first apartment for a year. I was all by myself and she was all by herself. My grandpa passed away and she invited me to live with her. Here I am twenty-three, and I decided to move in with my seventy-year-old gammy!

I lived with her for three years and we had this great relationship as roommates. I learned a lot from her on relationships. . . . She's brilliant and self-taught, well read, strong—and she taught me about social-emotional IQ. When I lived with her, she would get phone calls from people all the time, friends and family members asking for advice or guidance. I would ask her questions: 'Am I making the ethical right decision about things?'

The things she would value were very closely aligned to the things I had from my nuclear family, just faith and family and self-resiliency and independence, getting an education, having good relationships with people. But the other thing I really valued from her—the older I got, I learned how nonjudgmental she was. That open-mindedness. Every story comes with lots of different angles.

I have heard feedback from people that they appreciate that I will take time even when I am busy to just shut the door and listen to whatever it is that they have to share with me. I think that social-emotional piece has helped in my leadership style.

At seemingly different times in our lives—from the time I was twenty-three to twenty-six—we just really needed each other. At the time, it didn't seem like anything unique or different but, in reflecting, not too many people do that at that age. I know it was exactly what I needed, and she has since shared that that's what she needed at that time of her life too.

Natural mentors like Valerie's gammy have a rare opportunity to notice and amplify the importance of a girl's family values. When you detect a value referenced during a conversation, call her attention to it. "Oh, I can see from what you've just told me that honesty is important to you. That's one of your values." This may or may not spark additional values-centered conversation at the time. Regardless, you are adding values recognition—and appreciation—to your girl's toolkit of self-awareness.

Now she can consider and reflect on other values her family may live by and sift through them. Adolescence is a time a girl may reject some family values she disagrees with. (Major eye-rolling here.) It is also a time for her to choose values that represent who she is now as well as the Self she aspires to become on her journey. You are in a unique position to listen as she grapples with how to approach choosing values for herself.

As she gets older, she may realize some of those rejected family values are actually values she does want to live by. Help her understand that while her core values will probably remain constant throughout life, some values may increase or decrease in importance depending on the situation. For example, valuing learning and education may remain among her lifetime core values, but valuing "studying hard" may recede as her formal education yields to a career in which the need for studying may decrease.

Finally, never underestimate your power as a values role model. This is a case when your actions do speak louder than words. Consistently showing up in her life for events and activities you have planned together is a model of dependability. Authentically listening to her without interruption during conversations, thoughtfully reflecting back her words in an effort to truly understand, refraining from "preaching" or reframing the conversation so it becomes about you—all these are ways you are modeling compassion and kindness. Even without words, she sees you.

Authentic Voice

Find your voice;
Then listen to it.
Even when it shakes.
Especially then.
—Leigh Standley

When you look up the word "voice" in the dictionary, there are several meanings. One is the sound that comes out of your mouth when you open it and speak or sing. Another is the unique perspective a writer takes in storytelling. How do you know if you are using your authentic voice, coming from your heart, your inner self? How do you know you are "being you" when you speak and act?

Some children stay inside the protective wall they have built, hiding their tender inner selves from the outside world. Others venture out, showing the "appropriate" self, depending on who they are interacting with and the situation they find themselves. *If they feel safe, children will move between their inner and outer selves.*

Depending on their life experiences, they can learn to reveal more and more of their inner, tender selves as they grow and mature. Positive, loving experiences and people can assist this process of development. Too many negative experiences or even traumatic events can cause the tender self to retreat and hide from vulnerability for a long time, sometimes even a lifetime.

Adults who role model, care, and stay present in a child's life can greatly help her navigate the negatives. Anna, who spoke earlier in the chapter about values, also had a lot to say about the importance of voice to young girls.

Anna: The Importance of Voice

I feel like girls are taught to just sort of be quiet and are afraid to really ask for what they want, and afraid to fight for what they believe in, and just be a presence, and at the center of stuff. I think that's really important, for young girls in particular, to see a strong woman like Betsy is.

She was always a big proponent of, it doesn't matter how old you are, you can still have an impact. Kids are the people that are going to change the world. In terms of my own self-awareness, she really made me realize I had a voice and if I talked, people would listen to me.

She's taught me how to talk about difficult topics. When I worked with her (on Montessori Model United Nations), we did so much research on the topics we were assigned that we knew every single thing about them. . . . We knew every single thing about our country, every single thing about the way that our country viewed the issues. That was one way in which she helped me to find a voice, because I was armed with knowledge.

If I ever had somebody try and talk to me about it and try to just say, 'Oh, no, you're wrong,' I was able to always back up what I had to say and answer the questions. I think that's essential when you talk about something so important, to know what you're talking about.

I'm kind of the one person that has continued on the social justice route, and that's been my entire direction in life. Betsy was the person who inspired that. The experience changed my life and made me a better person. It's because of her that I felt like I had a voice and I felt like I could make a difference in the world around me.

Girls traditionally have been taught to be good, to be liked, to be kind, to be nice. Pressure to live this version of themselves from families, schools, teachers, and coaches undermines their power and can prevent them from reaching their potential as leaders. In today's world, the ability to express and manage a full range of emotions, to establish boundaries, and to assert themselves in the face of bullying are critical competencies for girls in becoming women.

Girls look to their friends and to the women in their life for inspiration in marshaling the courage to accept their vulnerability. With your support as her natural mentor, your girl can begin to recognize values that speak to her. Your values conversations can help her identify an array of values to consider for herself. Other adults in her life can serve as values role models as well. She will "try on" values as she begins to identify and discern personal core values. Once she pinpoints two or three personal core values, they will become the measuring stick by which she will begin to live and speak her authentic voice.

Ebb and Flow

We have so little faith in the ebb and flow of life, of love, of relationships.
We leap at the flow of time and resist in terror its ebb.
We are afraid it will never return.
We insist on permanency, on duration, on continuity;
when the only continuity possible in life, as in love,
is in growth, in fluidity—in freedom.
—Anne Morrow Lindbergh

When life events are in flow, we are going full throttle, moving forward in productive and satisfying ways that are meaningful to us. Our relationships feel richly rewarding; we find ourselves in sync with the people we love. As mentors, we may sense we are making a difference.

Then *poof!* For reasons unknown to us, in an eye-blink, things can ebb and come to what feels like a screeching halt. Our health may falter, we may lose a job, we decide to quit a project that was meaningful just a short time ago. Our relationship with the girl in our life may become distanced. She may be involved with time-consuming activities at school; she may have gone to college and become immersed in a new life. She may have found a new love interest! We feel left out and forgotten.

It is clear from the heartful stories in this book that women and girls have the capacity to share the deepest, most meaningful and lasting relationships. As the girls grow and their life situations change from middle school to high school to college to beginning a first career or moving up the ladder in an organization, the time and ability of women and girls to sustain the closeness of their natural mentoring relationship ebb and flow.

Months may speed by without face-to-face time together, but the women and girls I have spoken with tell me it is important stay in touch if there is a separation of any duration. When one of them reaches out, they may connect again in that easy way dear friends do after being separated. The meaningful conversations start anew, continuing like they were never apart. They text, they email, they telephone one another. They plan lunch and dinner dates for times they can get together in the same place at the same time. They may separate physically, but they are always connected in heart and spirit no matter where they are.

Like the women in this book, some of us are the lucky ones who have more than one mentor in our lives, and sometimes, we have multiple mentors at the same time. Mentors may enter a girl's life just when she needs her. Another situation may arise, like a quest to understand a career from the perspective of a professional woman who is willing to explain her work. Mentors may connect their girls with other women mentors in nurturing different aspects of a girl's life.

The point, of course, is to contribute to their growth in an environment of trust, by supporting their self-knowledge and celebrating their strengths and freedom to choose. As Kahlil Gibran writes in *The Prophet,*

Your children are not your children,
They are the sons and daughters of Life's longing for itself . . .
You may give them your love but not your thoughts,
For they have their own thoughts.
And their souls dwell in the house of tomorrow,
which you cannot visit, not even in your dreams.

When you are a natural mentor, you care about a girl and the woman she is becoming. Your loving presence may be exactly what she needs to grow in her self-leadership—and possibly into the kind of leader who encourages other leaders to change the world. She knows who she is. She knows where she is going. She surrounds herself with others who support her and build her up. She nurtures and supports those around her. She does change the world, her corner of it and potentially much more than that.

Your presence, along with her team of caring adults, help to form her GPS for life and encourage her to courageously show up in the world as the best Self she can be: herself.

CHAPTER 7

The Natural Mentoring
Reach

When the whole world is silent . . .
even one voice becomes powerful.
—Malala Yousafzai

Adolescent Transformation

When my daughter Erin was thirteen, curly hair was "in" among her friends. She began to believe that her beautiful, heavy, thick, and long hair required an updated look. She decided it should first be cut about three inches beneath her chin, and then, for the first time in her life, the front would be trimmed . . . into bangs.

Second, she would have curls! For her, this meant a "permanent wave"—a process of chemically inducing the frothy halo of curls she envisioned for herself. In the middle of motherly forewarnings about questionable results, as well as risks of chemically treating very thick hair, I decided to step back. She could make this momentous decision on her own.

133

Delighted, she called the hair salon herself for an appointment. Together we sat as she endured three hours of smelly transformation in the bustling salon. The astonishing outcome was everything I'd silently feared: a mixture of not-quite-curls and angular bends and sticks of hair that jutted awkwardly from a row on her forehead and hung in wavy clumps down the back of her head.

Erin's hair had always been her sleek, shiny crowning glory. She was horrified. Turning to me, she cried accusingly, *MOM! HOW COULD YOU HAVE LET ME DO THIS TO MY HAIR?*

Whether or not you're a parent, no doubt you have your own cringe-worthy stories about this baffling age. Adolescence. We get it. We've all been there. Dickens said it famously in another context: "It was the best of times; it was the worst of times." Mothers watch in awe as our sweet, adorable little ones transform into grown-up girls with womanly bodies but mostly still-childish ways. With best intentions and little real know-how, we role model and, step by step, teach our daughters to become adults. During this time, we freely envelop them in the security of our love and support. We remember our own younger selves and expect this support to be rejected at times.

Then the eye-rolling starts. So soon? What a jolt.

Even more bewildering, we uneasily feel this world our girls will inherit shifting beneath our feet. So many aspects of adolescence are different today. For one, as I have noted throughout this book, adolescence is an extended succession of more years than ever before. Although girls and young women have the most opportunities of any time in history, they also experience far more risks. They are in the midst of the stunning complexities of a changing world. They are also gobsmacked by emotional, physical, and personal changes of their own.

Our girls feel the world shifting beneath them right along with us, noticing with a mixture of excitement and fear the gradual disappearance of their familiar childhood world. An uncertain path to adulthood is weighed down with unknowns. The desire to move from the comfortable ways of childhood is strong, and they know in their gut it is time to move toward independence. There is no question our daughters need unconditional parental love, knowledgeable care, and guidance during this precarious period of growth and development.

Yet even with the advantage of involved parents in their corner, our girls need more. Beyond their moms and dads, girls require a network of caring adults in their lives to thrive and to progress confidently and authentically toward adulthood today. Although the physical changes of adolescence begin earlier today, teens model or act like adults more slowly. They have even turned the word "adult" into a verb and worry that "adulting" will thrust responsibilities upon them before they are ready.[1]

Technology is shaping this generation. This group is fixated on their smartphones and social media with well-researched and frequently alarming outcomes. The iPhone was introduced in 2007, the year today's thirteen-year-old adolescents were born. In 2015, two out of three US teenagers owned an iPhone, and in 2017, the average teen checked her phone more than eighty times a day. In the most recent Monitoring the Future 2013–2015 survey, high school seniors spent six hours a day with new media: an average of 2.5 hours a day texting on their cell phones, about 2 hours a day on the internet, 1.5 hours on electronic gaming, and about a half hour on video chat. In the same survey, eighth graders spent a total of five hours a day with new media. On a school day, that means nearly all of their leisure hours are spent with new media.[2]

Where is the face-to-face interaction in their lives? In the past, teens' friends were ever present in groups in parks, at the movies, at the mall. Today, teen social life is mostly conducted online. In 2015, 87 percent of twelfth-grade girls used social media sites almost every day. The number of teens who get together with their friends every day has been cut in half in the past fifteen years, with even steeper declines recently. For teens today, online friendships have replaced offline friendships.[3] Adult presence is critically needed as a way to teach adolescents social conversation and behaviors.

Teens who spend more time on screen activities are more likely to be unhappy, and the risk of unhappiness because of social media use is the highest for the youngest teens. Eighth graders who spend six to ten hours a week on social media are 47 to 56 percent more likely to be unhappy than those who don't. Despite this virtual and seemingly constant connectivity, they also feel lonely. The loneliest teens spend more time on social media and less time with their friends in person. As this occurs, life satisfaction drops with shocking speed.[4]

Do you think there is a connection with these statistics about technology and today's generation of teens, which is on the verge of the most severe mental health crisis for young people in decades? Our culture has bred a generation of teens who are contending with depression, higher risks of suicide, and diagnosable anxiety disorders.[5]

Research on the status of girls' well-being today points to a critical need for face-to-face adult involvement in their lives. The 2017 Girls' Index surveyed nearly eleven thousand girls in grades five through twelve across racial and ethnic groups from different socioeconomic backgrounds and geographic areas. The first-of-its-kind national survey was designed to develop a deeper understanding of the thoughts, experiences, perceptions, beliefs, behaviors, and attitudes of girls throughout the United States. Its goal was to learn about what we as adults can do to make the world better for girls.[6]

This survey's findings are closely aligned with longitudinal study findings in the paragraphs above. The girls' use of social media increases as they get older, and 61 percent of the girls surveyed say their parents never monitor their use of social media. Girls who spend the most time on technology are the least likely to say they have supportive friends to talk to about serious issues. Girls' confidence declines as they get older, and 46 percent of high school girls do not think they are smart enough for their dream career.[7]

The increasing complexity of girls' and young women's lives coupled with the self-imposed individuality of technology immersion makes adult intervention compulsory. If for *no other reason* than experiencing the warmth of heart-to-heart, face-to-face talks with a genuine human being who cares, girls and young women desperately need the social interaction.

There is good news—natural mentoring is happening organically already. The extraordinary women I interviewed for natural mentoring stories came forward with accounts of not only adult involvement in girls' lives but also affirmation, encouragement, and love. They spoke of positive role models, active listeners, and ethical, trustworthy women who earned—and kept—their trust. These women came from all walks of life. They are women like you and me.

Here, within their roles in the lives of the girls they chose to mentor, are more of their stories. As you read them, ask yourself whether you notice a deepening self-awareness in either the mentor or the one being mentored. Is the mentor in the story walking beside the girl or young woman on her journey to her highest Self? Can you recognize the transition phases in some or all of the stories? Do you see unfolding leadership development? Are these relationships empowering girls and young women to use their authentic voices?

Relatives as Natural Mentors

Grandmothers

Grandmothers are not only loving family members in the lives of girls. They can be role models and supportive natural mentors.

Jean was her first grandchild, and Ella wanted nothing more than a close relationship with her. They spent hours of quality time together—visits, overnights, and weekends.

Most of all, Ella "tuned in" and listened.

As Jean grew older, Ella continued to listen in a nonjudgmental way. This "sounding board" approach offered a safe space of feedback without repercussion that Jean needed to process tender thoughts about what was going on in her life.

Their conversations opened Jean to herself. Ella says:

She could have things she had said to me run back to her. How do you feel about this? Where will this take you if you do that? [These questions] made her think things through a little bit more. If she was trying something or working on something, I was just really supportive: you can do this.

Ella remarked how much she has learned from the close relationship with Jean.

I learned patience and acceptance, and I've learned to think about things from a different point of view. She is choosing a career that suits her so well [a hairdresser/salon owner].

The people we love are different human beings with their own personalities and their own self-concepts. We have to encourage that to allow them to grow into who they are meant to be.

Aunts

This sixty-plus-year-old natural mentoring story is close to my heart. The natural mentor is my mother, and her niece Sandy is my cousin. When

Mom was single and in her twenties, she lived in her childhood home with her mother and her sister's family. A baby girl—Mom's niece—was born during that time, and the close relationship they still share has lasted Sandy's whole life. When Sandy went to school, she wrote these words for an assignment:

> *My Aunt Marge has been the most influential woman in my life. From infancy through most of my childhood, she was always there, a loving, nurturing presence. She moved to Chicago over fifty years ago, but only the miles have ever separated us. Whenever I need her, she is only a phone call away and in some very dark moments of my life, she was by my side as quickly as possible.*
>
> *The lifelong lessons I have learned from her are many. She has taught me that each individual is special and that you can love someone even though you may not always condone their actions; that quality time with your loved ones far outweighs the material things in life; that kindness and compassion and encouragement need to be passed on to everyone possible; that listening is the key to communicating with others; that you 'judge not lest you be judged'; that a family is made of 'we' not 'I.'*
>
> *Aunt Marge has been my teacher, my champion, my confidant, my mentor, my confessor, my relative, my friend. Most of all, she has given me her unconditional love all the days of my life.*

Work Colleagues as Natural Mentors

Genevieve and Liz

Genevieve and Liz's story embodies the value of natural mentoring in the workplace. Theirs was not a formally matched mentoring relationship. It began and grew organically when Liz started her twenty-year career in accounting management.

That's where I met my first mentor, actually. I was in my early twenties. I had just graduated with my bachelor's degree. Up until that point, I really didn't have anyone in my life that was mentoring me. I didn't have a big sister. Certainly I had my mother, but it wasn't that close of a relationship at the time because when you're in your teens, it's your mom! I didn't have any aunts, no really strong women in my life, so it was really surprising to me.

When I went to work for a company, I was just a junior staff person, and this woman surfaced—from a different department! She was in her fifties, French, heavy French accent. I'm about six feet five. She was about four feet five.

Her name was Genevieve, and she took me under her wing. She certainly didn't have to, and I really didn't even realize it at the time. She saw something in me that I never even saw in myself. Probably within four months, I was promoted to accounting supervisor. When [the company] came to me, I was just totally floored. 'You want me to do what? I'm not a leader.'

It turns out that Genevieve had really gone to bat for me, and I didn't even realize that. From that point forward, I spent the next twenty years in leadership, leading people in teams, mentoring them, and developing them. Really, that was the one thing that saved me in the accounting world was working so closely with people.

I wondered how Liz and Genevieve first met, since they worked in different departments.

I think it was just through company luncheons. There weren't that many women, as I've found throughout my entire career, women in leadership roles. I've worked in different industries as well that are predominately male, so I think she did an excellent job of modeling for the young women in our accounting department.

She was extremely strong and spirited and would speak her mind. I had never worked with or actually been around a woman who was that confident and spoke her truth.

That was probably one of the biggest lessons that I took away from her when I was young: it is okay to speak your mind, to ask questions, and to challenge others with grace and respect.

I pretty much was the typical accountant back then, sitting in the cubicle, working on the spreadsheet, great smile but kept a lot to myself. When she approached me to give me the headsup that they're thinking about promoting me to supervisor, she probably saw the color drain from my face. I was like, 'Who, me?' and kind of looking over my shoulder like, 'Are you talking to me?'

She called me by my full name, of course, which not that many people ever have—I think two people in my entire life. She said, 'Elizabeth, people look up to you. They like you.'

I was just floored. Nobody had ever talked to me like that before. I was always the fun girl, the one that people liked, under the radar. I played sports. I played basketball in school. It was always about the team. It was never about me.

I remember being in meetings or listening to her speak to upper management and voicing her opinion or an opposite opinion than upper management. She did it respectfully but strongly and confidently [without] backing down. I really admired that. I had never been around . . . a female [who had spoken her truth this way], and so she really laid the groundwork for me about being a successful woman in the business world, breaking the ceiling, and having high expectations.

I can say this: whether I was in manufacturing, automotive, or technology, I really never felt like I was being kept down because

I was a woman because I was that confident and forthright in my communication about what I want, and I asked for what I wanted and needed. I guess I could never pull that card and say, 'They treated me that way because I'm a woman.'

When I reflect on it, I think women who face those barriers in the workplace and haven't been successful or really struggle in their environment, if we really peel back the layers, it's probably because they didn't have a strong woman mentor in business.

Judy and Pamela

Judy and Pamela have been in each other's lives for more than fifteen years. They met when Pamela interviewed Judy for a summer "before college" job after Judy graduated from high school. Their relationship has evolved from Pamela's mentoring Judy to mutual or peer mentoring and a warm, genuine friendship that continues today.

Judy remembered:

When you asked me if I have a mentor, Pamela sprang to my mind. I met her when I was seventeen through work. She actually interviewed me for the company I now work for as an executive assistant to my boss.

There was just something when I met her—she was very easy to talk to. Very fair. I saw her as a manager and she always examined everyone's perspective. I saw her as a decision maker, honest and very straightforward, which is how I am. Besides a mentor, she served as a role model for what it meant to be a professional, to work for a company, and how to handle yourself.

My relationship with Pamela taught me that people would listen to me. She opened my eyes to the fact that not everyone is like me. I think when you are a kid, you are not so aware that everyone is different and sees you differently and processes things differently.

She helped me realize it doesn't make other people wrong. That was a significant thing."

Pamela remembered too:

I just saw this person who was a little lost at the time, but she was so amazing. She had her act together as much as a seventeen-year-old possibly can. She's a hard worker, and I wanted to help her in any way I could. Honestly, I'm not like that with many people, but she was very special. She was such a good listener! . . . I felt like she wanted to know more. She's just special, and I wanted good for her. I thought of her like I would my little sister. The way that you would want your little sister to succeed and do well and be happy.

I think she has all of the traits that I respect in a person. She's a hard worker. She doesn't lie to you; she tells it like it is; she doesn't circle around whatever it is. . . . She doesn't blame other people. She takes responsibility. . . . Probably one of the biggest things I did for her or gave to her is I never, ever judge her. . . . She also doesn't judge me, but she can just be honest. She's straightforward. She's highly, highly organized. She has incredible energy.

I think there are people in her life—and I'm just one of them—that she has seen how they lead, and she respects it. It's a big misconception that if you're a female in the workforce, you need to lead or be a certain way. Realistically, all you need to do is earn respect. You earn respect working shoulder to shoulder with your team. I think that has left an impression on her.

And now, whoever needs the support at whatever time, we're there, unquestionably, anytime. It goes without saying, she knows that if she needs something, I will drop everything if she needed me to. I know the same for her, so I think there's comfort and strength in that, knowing that you have that person who is there.

Mary and Phyllis

Mary worked in a correctional institution, and Phyllis was her supervisor. Their natural mentoring relationship has continued for two decades. They both report the relationship evolved organically when they "just connected." Mary recalled Phyllis unexpectedly in the middle of telling me about her relationship as a natural mentor to Cassie.

Mary said:

> *This is reminding me I've had a natural mentor. I've had a mentor for twenty years. It's somebody that I worked with that saw something in me that I didn't see in myself.*

Phyllis remembered:

> *I believed Mary had a passion. She had a strong skill set, working with folks and wanting to learn. She was able to articulate treatment goals really well for them. She's a genuine, honest, and open person. When she started coming to me, I realized there were more opportunities that she should consider, being as young as she was and having the skills she has. She was passionate, kind, open, honest, but still very direct.*
>
> *We still talk, text. I don't think a mentor needs to be there physically. If either one of us had any difficulties or celebration moments, we would share those with one another.*

Older Friends as Natural Mentors to Younger Friends

Joan and Andi

Joan and Andi met when both lived in Michigan. Joan was offering a workshop on Julia Cameron's *The Artist's Way*, and Andi wanted desperately to participate. She was struggling financially, and Joan simply said, "Please come." She traded the workshop fee for Andi's administrative assistance, and a mutually satisfying natural mentoring relationship began.

Andi remembered:

It actually gave me a really great sense of accomplishment because she brought out strength and confidence in me. To help her out with something in exchange for doing the workshop, not just giving me a free handout, helped me feel like I had a purpose and that I earned it.

Joan is someone I connected with quickly, just clicked, and I remember it being a very fluid thing that automatically happened. That's always a great thing when two people can start off a relationship and the comfort level is already very relaxed together.

Joan was my mentor and seemed like a rock that I could lean on. With that, I feel like she helped me find the toughness or the resilience in me so I could overcome my fear of moving away from my small hometown into a bigger city where I could accomplish more things for myself.

Joan made me feel like I was good at something, and that was invaluable. I felt appreciated and recognized for what I can do, and that definitely helped my self-confidence. I would go to book readings with her or other activities. Even just spending time with her, our conversations were casual but productive; they were positive. She brought out the best in me so I could just be me. I found self-respect, learning to respect myself, and knowing what I deserve, but also getting that right back from other people as well.

Maybe she saw something in me that I didn't or that I just didn't feel like showing at the time. . . . She helped me find my voice in terms of, I am put here to do something better for the world and that's going to be my focus in life.

My hope for you is that you see yourself in these narratives and are inspired to share in the journey of a girl or young woman who is already, naturally in your life. Someone for whom you want the best. Someone you already care deeply about. Someone whose relationship with you stands to be one of the most important factors in helping her on her journey to grow into the woman you can already see within her.

Natural Mentors as Partners in Making the World a Better Place

In chapter 1's description of the Power2Thrive natural mentoring program, I introduced the idea of a "field experience." Natural mentors and girls delve into the many aspects of self-awareness together and become familiar with the workings of the adolescent brain. They explore the changes they are each experiencing through the transition process. Having an experiential grasp on what it means to lead from the inside out can also provide firsthand practice in speaking their authentic voice.

At this point in their enhanced relationship, natural mentors and girls know and care about each other's values and interests. This is prime time for natural mentors to tap into what girls are learning along their GPS journey by organically uncovering some issues greater than themselves. You do not have to be involved in a natural mentoring program to tap into personal and societal problems you are both already noticing. There may be broader, global issues like climate change and gender and racial equality. There may be closer-to-home community issues like water shortages, homelessness, not enough equipment on school playgrounds. There are also personal creative interests like art in its many forms: writing, drawing, painting, pottery, music, dance.

Pairs of natural mentors and girls can explore together the questions that remain unanswered for them about the near and far world around them. As you grapple with and formulate questions together, you are creating and may problem solve around areas of mutual interest. Thoughts and ideas will spring up about ways to solve specific problems you identify.

Over time, these thoughts can grow into strategies for solving the problems, creating the art, or building awareness around a community issue. Turning the strategies into a project together and planning how to take the project to completion can build confidence and self-efficacy in your girl as she realizes she has the power to make a difference. It is a way to connect even more deeply with each other, as well as to introduce your girl to other caring adults who are also committed to tackling the issues you have identified.

In a corner of my heart, there is a clear vision of a world in which pairs of girls and adult women are deeply connected. Together with the girls' parents, guardians, or caretakers, they form a network of love and support around girls that is impenetrable. The pairs are meaningful to each other and extraordinarily significant to the quality and trajectory of their lives. They see each other wholly, fully—warts and all. They feel each other completely. They have each other's back. They help each other make authentic connections, and they tell it like it is.

What if "natural mentor" were a household term that everybody recognized and embraced?

What if, like the women in the stories above, we are intentionally and actively present in the lives of the adolescents who are part of our world? What if we acknowledge and understand the central need for deeper relationships with the girls and young women we love, teach, and work with? What could the world be like if we each accept, embrace, and engage in a unique role that champions at least one girl or one young woman?

CHAPTER *8*

What's Next?

Beginning Your Natural Mentoring Journey

> I am still every age that I have been. Because I was once a child,
> I am always a child. Because I was once a searching adolescent,
> given to moods and ecstasies, these are still part of me, and always
> will be. Because I was once a rebellious student, there is and always
> will be in me the student crying out for reform. This does not mean
> that I ought to be trapped or enclosed in any of these ages, but that
> they are in me to be drawn on . . .
> —Madeleine L'Engle, *A Wrinkle in Time*

So, it's dawning on you. Yes, there is a girl or young woman in your life. She is your niece, or your friend's daughter, or your student, or your children's babysitter, or your colleague.

Maybe she is a lone petunia in her family garden. Maybe not.

Regardless, you see something in her. You're not sure she sees herself in the ways you do. It's time, you realize, to do your part in helping her develop as she reaches toward becoming the woman she is meant to be.

A thrill travels up your spine. This is going to be fun!

Then you stop. Your mind goes blank.

What do you do first? Where do you begin?

Read on.

An Action Plan to Get Started

Who Are YOU?
Using the Thrive Cycle
to Deepen Your Own
Self-Awareness

Embrace the Thrive Cycle. Use it to grasp and claim your capacity to be a natural mentor. Whether you realize it or not, you have reached this point in your life by journeying in your own unique way through each of the five Thrive Cycle components. The cycle is part of lifelong learning, and it never ends until we do!

You may be wondering about your natural mentoring capability. Whether you feel hesitant and uncertain or confident and eager to begin, the following section is intended to help you dig deep inside yourself and see clearly how far you've come and how much you've learned about life.

I invite you to carve out a few hours, a day, or a weekend of self-care time. Engage in some delicious life reflection!

Begin by reading through the prompts listed below each Thrive Cycle component. Use them to recall your life experiences as you remember them. Better yet, start a journal and write your responses. This will provide you a written record to connect with your own life—time and time again.

Thrive Cycle Component 1
Become "Whole Self" Aware

    a. Use the list of key terms on page 22 in chapter 2 to help you visualize a timeline of your emerging "young girl" sense of self to your sense of self as the person you are today. Draw a line in your journal and place the timeline on it.

b. In mulling over the many aspects of self in the list, what life experiences and situations contributed to your growing self-awareness? Write briefly about some that stand out for you.

c. What people in your standout life experiences contributed to a growing realization of your "whole self"? Write a few sentences about these special people.

d. Do some pre-mentor thinking by responding to the ten questions on pages 26 and 27 in chapter 2.

e. Take a look at the Authentic Listening Touchstones on pages 36 and 37 in chapter 2. Can you think of a person or persons in your life who listened authentically to you? Jot down what "feeling heard" meant to you.

Thrive Cycle Component 2
Keep the Brain in Mind

a. Can you think of some ways your significant relationships helped you make sense of your experiences? List ways they helped or did not help.

b. Now that you are familiar with the Triangle of Well-Being on page 49 in chapter 3, which relationships contributed to your feelings of well-being—or not? Write a few of these down.

c. Thinking about the Hand Model of the Brain (page 61 in chapter 3), reflect on one or two notable times in your life when your emotions got the better of you, when you *reacted* and may regret that now. How might you have *responded* differently if you had known about the physiology of a meltdown during those times? Ponder these thoughts and briefly rewrite your reactive memory into a responsive story instead.

d. Think of your adolescent years and the quest for independence. Can you remember experiences you had that demonstrated some or all of the qualities of mind Dr. Siegel identified in the changing adolescent brain (chapter 3, pages 63 through 68)—novelty seeking, social engagement, increased emotional intensity, and creative exploration)? Jot down one or two of the experiences that popped into your mind.

e. Describe your mindfulness practice. If you don't practice mindfulness, write some thoughts on how you might build such a practice into your life.

f. During this self-care time, reread the Wheel of Awareness meditation that begins on page 72 in chapter 3. Consider how you might incorporate this as a useful tool in your life and jot down a few thoughts.

Thrive Cycle Component 3
Celebrate Change and Transition

a. Take a few minutes to review the timeline you drew about your emerging sense of self. Using the same timeline, think of a few significant change events in your life. Put these changes on your timeline. When did these changes occur as your sense of self was maturing? Was there any alignment? Jot down a few thoughts about this.

b. Consider the change events you just wrote about. How might you have navigated each of them differently if you had known about the process of transition? Briefly rewrite (or simply think about) one of the most significant change events as though you had been aware of using all or parts of the 4S process on pages 88 and 89 in chapter 4 to help you through it. Reflect on the difference this might have made.

c. Reflect on your strengths. It may be helpful to Google "personal strengths" or take a look at the Clifton34 list of strengths on the Gallup website to help you.[1] (A link appears in the Notes section under chapter 8.) Write down your top two or three strengths. Are you aware of your character strengths? If you have time, you can learn what they are by taking the short (free) VIA Character Strengths survey.[2] (A link appears in the Notes section under chapter 8.) This survey will let you see which of the twenty-four character strengths are your "signature strengths."

Thrive Cycle Component 4
Lead from the Inside Out

a. Think about the current state of our world. In what ways are volatility, uncertainty, complexity, and ambiguity apparent in your ordinary life?

b. Personal leadership—leading yourself first—is another way of thinking about self-regulation. As you consider your own journey of personal leadership, what experiences in your life presented opportunities to lead yourself first?

c. What life experiences can you remember that enabled you to demonstrate one-to-one or private leadership? Think about friendships, family, or work relationships.

    d. How have you drawn from self-awareness, your strengths, and your relationships to exercise public leadership (one to many) in your life? As you think back, how have these experiences contributed to your self-mastery?

Thrive Cycle Component 5
Find and Use Your Authentic Voice

    a. Have you experienced the feeling that your social self is different from your authentic self—who you are inside, at your core? What was happening in your life when you felt that way?

    b. When did you begin to feel safe revealing your authentic self? Write down this story briefly so you can remember it. (Do you feel safe? If not, write about that.)

    c. How have your values evolved over time? What about your core values? You can explore values more thoroughly by Googling "values" and choosing a free values assessment.[3] (There is a link to three of these in the Notes section under chapter 8.)

    d. Can you remember when you first used your voice to express yourself? Write down this experience from your memory.

Who Is SHE?
Using the Thrive Cycle in Your Natural Mentoring Role

How do you feel after thinking back on your life through the lens of each Thrive Cycle Component? Are you getting the sense that your memorable life experiences and "big feels" may have value for someone else? If your "someone else" is a girl or young woman who is already in your life, picture her face as you move forward with the worthy idea of sharing her journey to adulthood.

But wait. What if your heart is ready but there is no girl or young woman who is naturally in your life? If this is the case and you feel the pull to mentor, think about these girl-serving organizations and individuals for ideas:

a. Friends who are parents
b. Your local church
c. School counselors
d. Girls in Action
e. Big Brothers and Big Sisters
f. Girls, Inc.
g. Girls on the Run
h. Corporations that have established mentoring programs

Talk with adults and representatives from these or other teams and organizations you may know about. Become involved as a volunteer in one or two organizations that interest you. As you come to know the girls and young women, one or two may surface who capture your interest and, in time, your heart.

Now the time has come to embrace the Thrive Cycle once again. Use its five components to encourage your own awareness for natural mentoring opportunities with your girl or young woman, such as:

A struggle she's experiencing
- at home
- with friends
- in school
- at the workplace

A transition time in her life
- middle school to high school
- high school to college
- initial stages of career to leadership roles

Traumatic life experience(s)

- a loss
- a nonevent (something she expected to happen or achieve that did not happen)
- an illness

Normal growth experiences

- adolescent issues
- initial career capabilities or occurrences

Your own life experiences

- Use this time to bridge generation gaps
- What life experiences of yours can illuminate hers?

Engage your girl or young woman in a few heart-to-heart conversations to determine her interest in establishing a deeper relationship. How can your relationship extend both ways and help each of you?

a. Explain your interest in the relationship

b. Discuss her interests

c. Listen to her version of life events

d. Ask open-ended questions

e. Listen to her responses

f. Discuss your interests

g. Listen as she asks you open-ended questions

h. Respond thoughtfully and reflectively

i. Allow time for separate thought and consideration

j. Listen and reflect what you hear her saying and what you sense her feeling

When it becomes clear you are both moving in a positive direction, ask her thoughts on becoming partners in your relationship. Have a conversation about the intersection of your interests and introduce the ideas around "reciprocal" or "mutual" mentoring. Is there something she can do for you so she feels the relationship is a two-way street? Would she like to provide technology assistance? Perhaps she can teach you something you've always wanted to learn? (Maybe she takes notes by mind-mapping or drawing pictures instead of writing down words. She could teach you this creative and brain-friendly method!)

You will want to speak with her parents or caregivers if she's under eighteen years of age. Explain your willingness to be there for her in this way. If parents or caregivers are unfamiliar with natural mentoring, share this book with them and explain the research-based importance of building a team of caring adults around their daughter.

When you have secured her parents' or caregivers' approval, the two of you can set mutual goals for your evolving relationship.

Set ground rules and regulations:
- How often will you want to meet face to face?
- Phone and text regulations
- Where do you want to meet?
- What happens if one of you breaks a ground rule?

Determine what you both want from the relationship:
- Is there something specific she wants your help with?
  1. When you feel it is appropriate, show her the Thrive Cycle drawing.
  2. Is there a component of the Thrive Cycle she's interested in learning about or working on?
- Is there something you have noticed and can tell her about?
  1. Use the Thrive Cycle drawing to help you articulate your thoughts.
  2. Listen to her responses in an openhearted, nonjudgmental way.

Tell her about your valuable self-care time in working through the Thrive Cycle components for yourself. Use the Thrive Cycle drawings to explain how you deepened your own self-awareness and begin to make a plan for her to do the same.

Together, work on revising the prompts at the beginning of this chapter under each Thrive Cycle component to reflect the age and stage of your girl or young woman.

Set initial goals for your time together, depending on her interests, age, and stage. A simple SWOT (Strengths, Weaknesses, Opportunities, Threats) Analysis can help steer you in the direction that makes the most sense for her self-perceived needs at this time:

- Develop small steps you can take toward goal achievement.
- Develop a timeline.
- Plan how you'll celebrate when goals are achieved.
- Goal setting and achievement will take on a life of its own. Continue the pattern of setting the goal, developing small steps with a timeline, and celebrating successes.

My heartfelt wish is that you enjoy this time together to the fullest. Laugh and cry together. Learn from each other. See the world through one another's eyes. Catch each other's excitement and enthusiasm. You're on your way!

A mentor is someone who allows you to see the hope inside yourself.

—Oprah Winfrey

With Gratitude

In the past decade, hardly a day has passed without the words "natural mentoring" rising in my heart and mind. Countless selfless souls have listened graciously, actively, reflectively, and lovingly to the ideas, emotions, words, and frustrations that poured out, from the deepest parts of me, on this topic.

You know who you are. We've held passionate conversations. I've talked nonstop, barely pausing between sentences. You've offered many gifts: your good humor, your expertise, your sincere interest, and your kind and patient presence. My gratitude overflows. I'll do my level best to personally thank each of you, but if I miss anyone, know that in no way does this omission diminish my grateful acknowledgement of the role you continue to play in bringing the concepts of natural mentoring to kitchen table conversations everywhere.

My midlife graduate school experience is as good a place as any to begin. It placed me firmly in the self-awareness and change components of the Thrive Cycle, in a space of coming to truly know myself for the first time. I am grateful to Dr. Christopher Washington and the experience of teaching at Franklin University, where I initially realized *everyone* needs self-exploration and self-awareness much earlier in life than graduate school.

Additional gratitude to Dr. Bob Norton, whose work with job analysis and curriculum development gave rise to my own. Thanks, Bob, for taking a chance on hiring me to help train trainers worldwide as part of my consulting career, work that still feeds my soul and helps pay the bills today. Thanks, too, to my colleague John Moser and his wife, Kathy, for our work together and the friendship that grew from it.

As time went on and natural mentoring ideas began to form, Andrea Dowding was the first to listen and reflect back what she heard. Thank you for your openness, advice, and love. Heartfelt thanks as well to the women who came together as a focus group to offer their presence and their consultation around ways to move forward with Power2Thrive natural mentoring workshop ideas: Jenn Bajec, Virginia Barney, Pat Wynn Brown, Jerry Browning, Nan Katzenberger, Karen Eisenbach, Jilaine Fewell, Mary Ellen Jones, Jane O'Loughlin, Mary B. Relotto, Susan Jasbeck Steinberg, and Ellen Moss.

These ideas would have never taken root if not for seeds planted by my mother, Margaret, and her lifelong natural mentoring relationship with my cousin Sandy Litzenberger. I am beyond grateful to both, as well as to my father, William, who would have been thrilled to hold a book in his hands written by his daughter. Miss you, Dad.

My son, Ryan, and daughter, Erin, ignited the fire of a mother's love when they were born, and I am grateful beyond measure for the closeness we share today now that they are grown with families of their own. Thank you both for my grandchildren, first Emily and now Sam, who are living, breathing reasons for doing this work. I am also deeply grateful for my close-knit family of siblings Julie, Bill, and Adrienne, and my nieces and nephew, who brought natural mentoring relationships into my life before I knew the term existed. The relationships I have with my siblings' children mirror the type of mutual love and caring respect I can envision in all natural mentoring relationships.

I am especially grateful for my merged family, created when my husband, Steve, and I decided to marry. Thank you to Stacy and Andy for openheartedly welcoming me into your life. I am grateful for both of you and the families you are raising with so much love. Rylan, Avery, Jake, and Mia add breadth and depth to our life and provide four more beautiful examples of the necessity for this work.

Deep gratitude extends to Rhonda Ware, who as director of the Alverno College Research Center for Women and Girls, introduced me to Dr. Nancy Athanasiou. Their belief in natural mentoring resulted in the development of pre- and post-workshop assessments to measure the impact of Power2Thrive.

Thanks to my Spaces for Change colleagues and friends LeAnne Grillo and Elayne Dorsey, whose help and support during Power2Thrive pilots were far above my expectations. Our Camp Snowball work with adult educators and their students greatly informed my practical understanding of systems thinking.

I extend profound thanks and utter respect to the people whose expertise has informed this book: Dr. Dan Siegel for twenty-eight exceptional hours of immersion with you in interpersonal neurobiology, the teenage brain, and the Wheel of Awareness; James Scouller for your leadership model, Dr. Peter Senge for all manner of systems thinking; Dr. William Bridges posthumously for increasing my understanding of change and transition; Dr. Jean Rhodes for your work at the Center for Evidence-Based Mentoring; Dr. Carol Dweck for your work with mindset; Dr. Daniel Goleman for the foundations of emotional intelligence; Dr. Parker Palmer for all your work, particularly circles of trust and touchstones for listening; Dr. Lisa Damour for help with the Notes section of this book; Dr. Verna Price for your time in graciously meeting with me and for insights about your highly acclaimed *Girls in Action* program; countless authors of books about women and adolescent girls; and organizations serving girls in the United States and around the world. Any errors I may have made in writing about your work are strictly mine and I take full responsibility.

Thank you from the bottom of my heart to the fifty women who sat and talked with me about both sides of natural mentoring, whether they experienced mentoring or served as a mentor (or both). I was totally unprepared for the level of their involvement and commitment to this process, and for the number who offered multiple names of women for me to contact. The interviews could have continued indefinitely. We engaged in face-to-face interviews, FaceTime interviews, and Skype interviews. Each interview exceeded an hour, although I always promised to cut it off at the sixty-minute mark. They were eager and willing to say more, say it from their hearts, and say it with love. Their names have been changed in their stories to protect their identities, but I know each one of them. Thanks again.

Heartfelt gratitude to five women without whom this book would never have been completed: The Sisters Collective. They are Julie Ashley, Kimichelle Bain, Anne Cox, Ilene Levinson, and Saralise Ward. Their support, suggestions, patience, and excitement have kept me going long after I felt like quitting. I love you ladies. You rock!

Thank you to my talented artist-educator-graphic facilitator—and best of all, friend—Sherill Knezel, whose illustrations grace this book cover and pages with her line, perspective, and heart.

Special thanks to Mary Yamin-Garone for reviewing first drafts of this book.

Much gratitude for creatively and strategically helping me set a path for this work, Christy Tryhus. Merida Johns, thank you for your responsive, open, and candid consultation around the mysteries of publishing. Jennifer Louden, thank you for sharing your writing experiences in such a warm and human way. All three of you made a difference for me in the writing process.

My flawless editor Megan Grennan asked the most pertinent questions, poked the bear in a wonderful way, helped me see without telling me what to see, and is truly the reason you are holding this book in your hands. She is also my niece and I love her dearly. A trillion thanks, Megan.

Finally, endless gratitude to the man I love, who shopped and cooked while I wrote, who understood when I needed more time, who made me laugh when it would have been easier to resort to tears. That man is my husband. Thank you, Steve. I owe you.

Notes

Introduction

1   Gloria Steinem, *The Truth Will Set You Free, But First It Will Piss You Off!* (New York: Random House, 2019).

Chapter 1

1   Seth Godin, "You've Arrived." *Seth's Blog.* July 30, 2017, https://seths.blog/2017/07/youve-arrived/.

Seth is a writer and marketing guru whose wildly popular blog comes into my inbox daily. When I considered writing about a "GPS for life," Seth's words drove home the importance of intention and support along the journey from current self to future Self. Visit his blog to read his cogent and conversation-provoking thoughts on change, leadership, education, and the spread of ideas.

2   Bob Johansen, *Leaders Make the Future* (San Francisco: Berrett-Koehler Publishers, Inc., 2012); *The New Leadership Literacies* (Oakland: Berrett-Koehler Publishers, Inc., 2017).

Bob is a distinguished fellow with the Institute for the Future in Silicon Valley. By observing and identifying ten world trends in the current decade, he named ten leadership skills required of future leaders and further developed them into leadership literacies. Leading ourselves is a first step in developing these critical literacies in ourselves and others. Bob observes what is known—that young people will become leaders in the future. *How* they will lead—and toward what outcome—is yet unknown. We can walk beside them as they become the adults they were meant to be. Learn more at http://www.iftf.org/bobjohansen/.

3   CDC, "QuickStats: Suicide Rates for Teens, 15–19 Years, by Sex, United States 1975–2015," *MMWR Morb Mortal Weekly Rept 2017*, 66 (2017): 816, http://dx.doi.org/10.15585/mmwr.mm6630a6.

4   Lisa Hinkelman, *The Girls' Index: New Insights into the Complex World of Today's Girls* (Columbus: ROX Ruling Our Experiences, 2017).
     The Girls' Index is a first-of-its-kind large-scale national survey designed to develop a deeper understanding of the thoughts, experiences, perceptions, beliefs, behaviors, and attitudes of teen girls throughout the United States. Read the report at https://rulingourexperiences.com/the-girls-index-report. ROX stands for Ruling Our Experiences and began in Columbus, Ohio, in 2006 as the research study of founder and executive director Dr. Lisa Hinkelman. Funding received in 2018 established the ROX Research and Training Institute. Its mission is to create generations of confident girls who control their own relationships, experiences, decisions, and futures. Learn more at https://rulingourexperiences.com/about-the-rox-institute.

5   J. Breslau, S. E. Gilman, B. D. Stein, T. Ruder, T. Gmelin, and E. Miller, "Sex Differences in Recent First-Onset Depression in an Epidemiological Sample of Adolescents," *Translational Psychiatry* 7, no. 5 (May 2017): e1139.

6   CIGNA, Ipsos, *CIGNA US Loneliness Index: Survey of 20,000 Americans Examining Behaviors Driving Loneliness in the United States*, 2018, https://www.cigna.com/assets/docs/ newsroom/loneliness-survey-2018-full-report.pdf?WT.z_ nav=newsroom%2Floneliness-survey%3BBody%3BView%20 the%20full%20survey%20report.

7   National Scientific Council on the Developing Child, *Supportive Relationships and Active Skill-Building Strengthen the Foundations of Resilience: Working Paper 13*, 2015, https://developingchild. harvard.edu/resources/supportive-relationships-and-active-skill-building-strengthen-the-foundations-of-resilience/.

The mission of the Center on the Developing Child at Harvard is to drive science-based innovation that achieves breakthrough outcomes for children and families. This multidisciplinary team seeks transformational impacts on lifelong learning, behavior, and physical and mental health. It draws on local, national, and international innovation in policy and practice focused on children and families. The Center designs, tests, and implements ideas in collaboration with a broad network of research, practice, policy, community, and philanthropic leaders. Its resource library is a treasure trove of useful information for caring adults about topics such as child development, resilience, brain-building, and motivation. Visit the resource library at https://developingchild.harvard.edu/ resources/.

8   E. C. Roehlkepartain, K. Pekel, A. K. Syvertsen, J. Sethi, T. K. Sullivan, and P. C. Scales, *Relationships First: Creating Connections That Help Young People Thrive* (Minneapolis: Search Institute, 2017).

The Search Institute is a nonprofit organization that studies and works to strengthen youth success in schools, youth programs, families, and communities. It bridges research and practice to help young people be and become their best selves. The Search Institute believes children and adolescents are powerful agents of change and, together with adults who listen to them, can be leaders in transforming communities and society. Learn more at https://www.search-institute.org/about-us/.

9   Leonard Sax, *Girls on the Edge: The Four Factors Driving the New Crisis for Girls* (New York: Basic Books, 2010).

10 E. Debold, L. M. Brown, S. Weseen, and G. K. Brookins, "Cultivating Hardiness Zones for Adolescent Girls: A Reconceptualization of Resilience in Relationships with Caring Adults," in *Beyond Appearance: A New Look at Adolescent Girls*, eds. N. G. Johnson, M. C. Roberts, and J. Worell (Washington: American Psychological Association, 1999), 181–204.

In this book chapter, the authors rethink resilience and introduce hardiness. They consider positive relationships with significant adults in girls' lives as potential "hardiness zones." These are defined as "spaces of real engagement and opportunities for girls to experience control, commitment, and challenge. Such hardiness zones move the focus from the individual girl to the network of relationships that create girls' social worlds and environments, allowing girls access to skills, relationships, and possibilities that enable them to experience power and meaning." Read the chapter at https://psycnet.apa.org/record/1999-02580-007.

11 P. L. Benson, *Parent, Teacher, Mentor, Friend: How Every Adult Can Change Kids' Lives* (Minneapolis: Search Institute, 2010).

12 National Scientific Council on the Developing Child, *Supportive Relationships and Active Skill-Building Strengthen the Foundations of Resilience: Working Paper 13*, 2015, https://developingchild. harvard.edu/resources/supportive-relationships-and-active-skill-building-strengthen-the-foundations-of-resilience/.

13 L. Steinberg, *Age of Opportunity: Lessons from the New Science of Adolescence* (New York: Houghton Mifflin Harcourt, 2014).
    Dr. Laurence Steinberg is a world-renowned expert on adolescence. This book explains the lengthening of adolescence and the implications of new research on what we know about the brain. The plasticity of the adolescent brain presents a crucial time for the brains of young people to change in positive and negative ways through experience and relationships.

14 S. Marsh, "Teenagers on Loneliness: 'We Want to Talk to Our Parents. We Need Their Guidance.'" *Guardian*, April 8, 2017, https://www.theguardian.com/society/2017/apr/08/teenagers-loneliness-social-media-isolation-parents-attention.

15 D. B. Murphey, Tawana Bandy, Hannah Schmitz, and Kristin Anderson Moore, *Caring Adults: Important for Positive Child Well-Being*, 2013, https://www.childtrends.org/publications/caring-adults-important-for-positive-child-well-being.

Chapter 2

1   E. A. Impett, "Girls' Relationship Authenticity and Self-Esteem Across Adolescence," *Developmental Psychology* (2008): 722–733.

2   C. Dweck, *Mindset: The New Psychology of Success* (New York: Ballantine Books, 2007).

Carol Dweck is a Stanford University professor whose research identified two ways individuals perceive their abilities to learn: those whose brain has a fixed mindset and those with a growth mindset. Teaching people about the differences between the two and the importance of the growth mindset to relationships and success in education, sports, and business has become Dr. Dweck's lifelong contribution. Many schools around the world teach parents and students ways to embody the growth mindset. For more information about the basics of mindset, visit https://www.mindsetkit.org/topics/about-growth-mindset.

The NeuroLeadership Institute, led by Dr. David Rock, researches and teaches about building a growth mindset culture in business. To learn more, click here: https://neuroleadership.com/your-brain-at-work/growth-mindset-culture-master-class.

3   D. Goleman and R. E. Boyatzis, "Emotional Intelligence Has 12 Elements. Which Do You Need to Work On?" *Harvard Business Review*, February 6, 2017, https://hbr.org/2017/02/emotional-intelligence-has-12-elements-which-do-you-need-to-work-on.

With his 1995 book *Emotional Intelligence,* Dr. Daniel Goleman illuminated the benefit of identifying and naming the emotions a person is feeling. We all feel emotions to help us focus and pay attention to what we are experiencing. We can learn to focus our attention and redirect heightened, inappropriate reactions to emotions. We can learn to pause and intentionally decide how to respond instead. This is the beginning of becoming emotionally intelligent. Today, emotional intelligence is taught around the world to adults and to children in schools in SEL—Social-Emotional Learning—programs. Learn more at https://www.6seconds.org/emotional-intelligence/get-started-emotional-intelligence/.

4   M. K. Garringer, *Elements of Effective Practice for Mentoring, 4th Edition* (Boston: MENTOR: The National Mentoring Partnership, 2015).

Michael Garringer is the director of Knowledge Management at MENTOR: The National Mentoring Partnership. The MENTOR mission is "to fuel the quantity and quality of mentoring relationships for America's young people and to close the mentoring gap." There are a number of models for formal mentorship, which is a deliberate matching of adult mentors with primarily at-risk youth. Some of these models can include one-adult-to-one-child mentoring, group mentoring, and peer mentoring. Formal mentoring programs connect mentors and mentees and monitor their progress. Evidence-based practice, updated as research outcomes become available, better assures high quality and more positive outcomes for mentoring programs.

Natural mentoring occurs when two people are naturally in each other's lives (relatives, friends, teachers, colleagues). Knowledge of best mentoring practices in formal mentoring programs is helpful for a natural mentor, and since quality mentor training is a benchmark of effective formal mentoring, I reference MENTOR and the *Elements* publications as excellent resources for caring adults who want to deepen their relationships with one or more young persons. Review the *Elements* at https://www.mentoring.org/images/uploads/Final_Elements_ Publication_Fourth.pdf.

5 E. Hopper, "The Study of Authenticity," *HealthyPsych*, February 12, 2018, https://healthypsych.com/the-study-of-authenticity/.
   In this positive psychology article, Elizabeth Hopper reviews the literature on authenticity as a component of well-being.

6 Parker J. Palmer, "Circle of Trust Touchstones for Safe and Trustworthy Space." Adapted with permission from the Center for Courage and Renewal. http://www.couragerenewal.org/ touchstones/.

7 Peter M. Senge, *Schools That Learn: A Fifth Discipline Fieldbook for Educators, Parents and Everyone Who Cares About Education* (New York: Crown Business, 2012).
   Peter Senge's work with systems thinking and the learning organization began in the world of business and moved into school systems. This fieldbook is an excellent introduction to the five disciplines of the learning organization: personal mastery, shared vision, mental models, team learning, and systems thinking. It contains activities for individuals and schools and is a great resource for natural mentors and their girls and young women in seeking personal vision—the results you each want to create in your life.
   As your interest in systems thinking grows, The Waters Center is an excellent resource for you and your girl or young woman to learn more. Cultivating the Habits of a Systems Thinker presents ways to see our world as the interrelated system

of systems that it is. You can access The Waters Center here: https://waterscenterst.org.

8   C. Dweck, "Carol Dweck Revisits the Growth Mindset," *Education Week* (September 22, 2015): 20–24.

There is an excellent graphic in this *Education Week* article that explains how an adult can speak to a young person to encourage a growth mindset. The good news is that a growth mindset can be learned and nurtured. You can find the graphic at https://www.edweek.org/ew/articles/2015/09/23/carol-dweck-revisits-the-growth-mindset.html.

Watch Dr. Dweck's 2014 TED Talk about mindset at https://www.ted.com/talks/carol_dweck_the_power_of_believing_that_you_can_improve?language=en.

Chapter 3

1   D. J. Siegel, *Brainstorm: The Power and Purpose of the Teenage Brain* (New York: The Penguin Group, 2013).

In this chapter, I draw heavily from Dr. Daniel J. Siegel's book about the teenage brain, which illuminates teenage and adolescent behavior and the true physical reasons—and psychological implications—behind it. The other Siegel books in the list below are excellent resources if you want to delve more deeply into mindsight, the Wheel of Awareness and the inner workings of the mind.

I also draw from the work of Dr. Laurence Steinberg in his book below. Dr. Steinberg's conviction that the brain plasticity in adolecence presents a key time to develop self-regulation aligns seamlessly with a natural mentor's effort in nurturing a young person's competence and confidence. With support from caring adults, the childhood need for external control can gradually grow into the self-regulation required in adulthood.

Laurence Steinberg, *Age of Opportunity: Lessons from the New Science of Adolescence* (New York: Houghton Mifflin Harcourt, 2014).

2   D. J. Siegel, *Mindsight: The New Science of Personal Transformation* (New York: Bantam Books, 2011).

3   D. J. Siegel and T. P. Bryson, *The Whole Brain Child: 12 Revolutionary Strategies to Nurture Your Child's Developing Mind* (New York: Bantam Books, 2012).

4   D. J. Siegel, *Mindsight: The New Science of Personal Transformation* (New York: Bantam Books, 2011).

5   D. J. Siegel, *Mind: A Journey to the Heart of Being Human* (New York: W. W. Norton & Company, Inc., 2017).

6   D. J. Siegel and T. P. Bryson, *The Whole Brain Child: 12 Revolutionary Strategies to Nurture Your Child's Developing Mind* (New York: Bantam Books, 2012).

7   N. Herrmann and A. Herrmann-Nehdi, *The Whole Brain Business Book, Second Edition* (New York: McGraw-Hill, 2015).

8   D. J. Siegel and T. P. Bryson, *The Whole Brain Child: 12 Revolutionary Strategies to Nurture Your Child's Developing Mind* (New York: Bantam Books, 2012).

9   "Brain Development," First Things First, accessed March 27, 2019, https://www.firstthingsfirst.org/early-childhood-matters/brain-development/.

10 D. J. Siegel, *Mind: A Journey to the Heart of Being Human* (New York: W. W. Norton & Company, Inc., 2017).

11 D. J. Siegel, *Brainstorm: The Power and Purpose of the Teenage Brain* (New York: The Penguin Group, 2013).

12 J. Rhodes and E. Raposa, "Mentoring by the Numbers: Some Surprising Trends in Volunteer Efforts," *Chronicle of Evidence-Based Mentoring* (July 2017), https://www.evidencebasedmentoring.org/mentoring-numbers-surprising-trends-volunteer-efforts/.
    Dr. Jean Rhodes is a professor of psychology at the University of Massachusetts, Boston, where she serves as director of the Center for Evidence-Based Mentoring (https://www.rhodeslab.org/center-for-evidence-based-mentoring/). The goal of the center is to advance research in youth mentoring and make research outcomes more accessible to mentoring practitioners. Dr. Rhodes has devoted her career to understanding the role of intergenerational relationships in the lives of disadvantaged youth. You can subscribe to the center's newsletter, the *Chronicle of Evidence-Based Mentoring,* by clicking on the link above.

13 Laurence Steinberg, *Age of Opportunity: Lessons from the New Science of Adolescence* (New York: Houghton Mifflin Harcourt, 2014).

14 J. M. Twenge, *iGen: Why Today's Super-Connected Kids Are Growing Up Less Rebellious, More Tolerant, Less Happy—and Completely Unprepared for Adulthood* (New York: ATRIA Books, 2017).

15 D. J. Siegel and T. P. Bryson, *The Whole Brain Child: 12 Revolutionary Strategies to Nurture Your Child's Developing Mind* (New York: Bantam Books, 2012).

16 D. J. Siegel, *Brainstorm: The Power and Purpose of the Teenage Brain* (New York: The Penguin Group, 2013).

17 D. J. Siegel, *Brainstorm: The Power and Purpose of the Teenage Brain* (New York: The Penguin Group, 2013).

18 J. P. Shatkin, *Born to Be Wild: Why Teens Take Risks, and How We Can Keep Them Safe* (New York: Penguin Random House LLC, 2017).

19 Global EQ Community, "How to Practice Emotional Intelligence," Six Seconds, accessed November 25, 2018, https://www.6seconds.org/2018/03/28/emotional-intelligence-tips-choice/.

The 6seconds.org website is an excellent resource to begin to learn about EQ or emotional intelligence. It contains practical skills and a free e-book to help you put EQ into action.

20 G. Biegel, "Mindfulness-Based Stress Reduction for Teens (MBSR-T)," Stressed Teens, https://www.stressedteens.com/training-for-professionals.

This online training for educators, sports coaches, and counselors focuses on mindfulness for adolescents. It is based on the Mindfulness-Based Stress Reduction (MBSR) Program created by Jon Kabat-Zin, founder of the Center for Mindfulness in Medicine, Health Care, and Society at the University of Massachusetts Medical School.

21 APA, *Stress in America* (Washington: American Psychological Association, 2014).

22 D. Divecha, "Our Teens Are More Stressed Than Ever: Why, and What Can You Do About It?" *Developmental Science* (May 2019), https://www.developmentalscience.com/blog/2019/5/7/our-teens-are-more-stressed-than-ever.

23 Marina Khidekel, "10 Mindfulness Habits That Will Make You More Successful at Work," *Thrive Global* (March 2019), https://thriveglobal.com/stories/mindfulness-tips-habits-success-focus-work/.

Arianna Huffington is the founder and CEO of *Thrive Global* (https://thriveglobal.com), a company focused on the science of behavior change to help individuals, corporations, and communities make the connection between well-being and performance. The Thrive Global website and newsletter offer useful and practical resources. Its newsletter frequently solicits ideas from readers at home and at work.

24 D. J. Siegel, *Mindsight: The New Science of Personal Transformation* (New York: Bantam Books, 2011).

25 D. J. Siegel, *Mindsight: The New Science of Personal Transformation* (New York: Bantam Books, 2011).

26 D. J. Siegel and T. P. Bryson, *The Whole Brain Child: 12 Revolutionary Strategies to Nurture Your Child's Developing Mind* (New York: Bantam Books, 2012).

Additional Resources for Exploring the Brain and Mindfulness

X. V. Dzung, *The Mindful Teen: Powerful Skills to Help You Handle Stress One Moment at a Time* (Oakland: Instant Help: An Imprint of New Harbinger Publications, Inc., 2015).

This book is a resource written simply and clearly to and for teens by a pediatrician who specializes in adolescent health and wellness. It is a distillation of his own experiences with Zen master Thich Nhat Hanh, as well as with leaders and teachers in the fields of mindfulness, mental health, and positive youth development. Its wise and empathic chapters offer mindfulness-based techniques that truly resonate with teens.

The *Greater Good Science Center* (https://greatergood. berkeley.edu/) studies the psychology, sociology, and neuroscience of well-being and teaches skills that foster a thriving, resilient, and compassionate society.

Hey Sigmund (https://www.heysigmund.com) is an engaging website that contains news and information about research in psychology as it impacts life and the human mind. Its author is a psychologist who lives in Australia.

Mindful (https://www.mindful.org/) is dedicated to inspiring, guiding, and connecting anyone who wants to explore mindfulness.

MindShift (https://www.kqed.org/mindshift/) is a free editorially independent source of education news and information serving teachers and parents around the world. *MindShift* is a service of NPR/PBS member station KQED.

MindUP (https://mindup.org) is a neuroscience-based program offered for home and school. The *MindUP* curriculum begins with the brain and teaches the skills and knowledge children through eighth grade need to regulate stress and emotion, form positive relationships, and act with kindness and compassion. *MindUP* was founded by the Goldie Hawn Foundation.

Chapter 4

1   Bob Johansen, *Leaders Make the Future* (San Francisco: Berrett-Koehler Publishers, Inc., 2012); Bob Johansen, *The New Leadership Literacies* (Oakland: Berrett-Koehler Publishers, Inc., 2017).

Bob is a distinguished fellow with the Institute for the Future in Silicon Valley. I chose to begin the chapter on change with a broad exploration of the state of the world. Bob's clear explanation of our VUCA world—volatile, uncertain, complex, and ambiguous—as well as the disturbing recognition that these constant changes are increasing rather than going away are important concepts for everyone to grasp. Forming a clear picture of the changes we face both inside and outside ourselves is essential in moving through the process of transition during each of them. When it comes to the world's unprecedented changes, both adults and young people face them together. Learn more at http://www.iftf.org/bobjohansen/.

2   William B. Bridges and Susan Bridges, *Managing Transitions: Making the Most of Change* (Philadelphia: Da Capo Press, 2016).

3   M. G. Anderson, *Counseling Adults in Transition: Linking Schlossberg's Theory with Practice in a Diverse World* (New York: Springer Publishing Company, 2012).

4   National Scientific Council on the Developing Child, *Supportive Relationships and Active Skill-Building Strengthen the Foundations of Resilience: Working Paper 13,* 2015, http://www.developingchild.harvard.edu.

The mission of the Center on the Developing Child at Harvard is to drive science-based innovation that achieves breakthrough outcomes for children and families. This multidisciplinary team seeks transformational impacts on lifelong learning, behavior, and physical and mental health. It draws on local, national, and international innovation in policy and practice focused on children and families. The Center designs, tests, and implements ideas in collaboration with a broad network of research, practice, policy, community, and philanthropic leaders. Its resource library is a treasure trove of useful information for caring adults about such topics as child development, resilience, brain-building, and motivation. Visit the resource library at https://developingchild.harvard.edu/resources/.

5   A. Mitchinson and Robert Morris, *Learning About Learning Agility* (Greensboro: Center for Creative Leadership, 2014).

6   R. M. Niemiec, *The Power of Character Strengths* (Cincinnati: VIA Institute on Character, 2019).

7   R. M. Niemiec, *The Power of Character Strengths* (Cincinnati: VIA Institute on Character, 2019).

8   R. M. Niemiec, "VIA Character Strengths: Research and Practice (The First 10 Years)," in *Well-Being and Cultures: Perspectives on Positive Psychology*, eds. H. H. Knoop and A. Delle Fave (New York: Springer, 2013), 11–30.

9   R. M. Niemiec, *The Power of Character Strengths* (Cincinnati: VIA Institute on Character, 2019).

Additional Resources for Living a Strengths-Based Life

The VIA Institute on Character is a nonprofit organization based in Cincinnati, Ohio, dedicated to helping people change their lives by tapping into the power of their own greatest strengths. In the early 2000s, scientists discovered a common language of twenty-four character strengths that we all possess in varying degrees. Learn more at https://www.viacharacter.org/character-strengths.

This means each one of us has a unique character profile. Since character strengths are building blocks to our identity, continuing to develop our own character strengths as we help young people learn and develop theirs is a mutually beneficial undertaking. To learn your top character strengths, if you are over eighteen years old, take the free survey at https://www. viacharacter.org/survey/account/register#adult.

A free survey is also available for youth ages 10–17 at https:// www.viacharacter.org/survey/account/register#youth.

Caring adults have a golden opportunity to help young people to identify their unique interests and talents. With continued support, young people can develop these unique talents into strengths that will help them succeed throughout life. As natural mentors model their own continued strengths development, they encourage and support their girls in taking a strengths-based approach to the journey to adulthood.

The well-respected Gallup Corporation offers a series of books and assessments to help young people and adults identify their top or "signature strengths." A list of the Gallup strenghs themes is at https://www.gallupstrengthscenter.com/home/en-us/ cliftonstrengths-themes-domains.

Gallup offers strengths assessments starting with the Clifton StrengthsExplorer for ten- to fourteen-year-olds at https://www. gallupstrengthscenter.com/home/en-us/strengthsexplorer.

Another strengths assessment for older students can be accessed through a code in the book CliftonStrengths for Students, accessible at https://www.strengthsquest.com/205382/ cliftonstrengths-students.aspx.

Chapter 5

1 B. Johansen, *Leaders Make the Future* (San Francisco: Berrett-Koehler, 2012).

2 B. Johansen, *Get There Early: Sensing the Future to Compete in the Present* (San Francisco: Berrett-Koehler, 2007).

3   B. Johansen, *The New Leadership Literacies* (Oakland: Berrett-Koehler, 2017).

4   B. Johansen, *Leaders Make the Future* (San Francisco: Berrett-Koehler, 2012). Learn more at http://www.iftf.org/bobjohansen/.

5   *Merriam-Webster Dictionary Online*, s.v. "volatile," accessed May 19, 2019, www.merriam-webster.com.

6   A. Mitchinson and Robert Morris, *Learning About Learning Agility* (Greensboro: Center for Creative Leadership, 2014).

7   J. Scouller, *The Three Levels of Leadership* (Oxford: Management Books, 2016).

8   J. Scouller, *The Three Levels of Leadership* (Oxford: Management Books, 2016).

9   J. Scouller, *The Three Levels of Leadership* (Oxford: Management Books, 2016).

10 D. Rock, *Handbook of NeuroLeadership* (London: NeuroLeadership Institute, 2013).

11 P. M. Senge, *The Dawn of System Leadership* (Stanford: Leland Stanford Jr. University, 2015).

Chapter 6

(no citations)

Chapter 7

1   J. M. Twenge, *iGen: Why Today's Super-Connected Kids Are Growing Up Less Rebellious, More Tolerant, Less Happy—and Completely Unprepared for Adulthood* (New York: ATRIA Books, 2017).

2   J. M. Twenge, *iGen: Why Today's Super-Connected Kids Are Growing Up Less Rebellious, More Tolerant, Less Happy—and Completely Unprepared for Adulthood* (New York: ATRIA Books, 2017).

3   J. M. Twenge, *iGen: Why Today's Super-Connected Kids Are Growing Up Less Rebellious, More Tolerant, Less Happy—and Completely Unprepared for Adulthood* (New York: ATRIA Books, 2017).

4   J. M. Twenge, *iGen: Why Today's Super-Connected Kids Are Growing Up Less Rebellious, More Tolerant, Less Happy—and Completely Unprepared for Adulthood* (New York: ATRIA Books, 2017).

5   J. Anderson, "Coping Skills for Anxious Times," accessed November 29, 2017, www.gse.harvard.edu.

6   Lisa Hinkelman, *The Girls' Index: New Insights into the Complex World of Today's Girls* (Columbus: ROX Ruling Our Experiences, 2017).

7   Lisa Hinkelman, *The Girls' Index: New Insights into the Complex World of Today's Girls* (Columbus: ROX Ruling Our Experiences, 2017).

Chapter 8

1 Gallup, Clifton34, https://www.gallup.com/cliftonstrengths/en/253715/34-cliftonstrengths-themes.aspx.

2 To learn your top character strengths, if you are over eighteen years old, take the free survey at https://www.viacharacter.org/survey/account/register#adult.

3 Barrett Values Centre, Personal Values Survey (PVS), https://www.valuescentre.com/tools-assessments/pva/

Carnegie Mellon University-Values Survey
https://www.cmu.edu/career/documents/my-career-path-activities/values-exercise.pdf

MindTools *What Are Your Values?* https://www.mindtools.com/pages/article/newTED_85.htm

Bibliography

Achor, Shawn. *The Happiness Advantage: How a Positive Brain Fuels Success in Work and Life.* New York: Currency, 2010.

American Psychological Association. *Stress in America.* Washington: American Psychological Association, 2014.

Anderson, M. G. *Counseling Adults in Transition: Linking Schlossberg's Theory with Practice in a Diverse World.* New York: Springer Publishing Company, 2012.

Anderson, J. "Coping Skills for Anxious Times." Harvard Graduate School of Education, November 29, 2017, https://www.gse. harvard.edu/news/uk/17/11/coping-skills-anxious-times.

Benson, P. L. *Parent, Teacher, Mentor, Friend: How Every Adult Can Change Kids' Lives.* Minneapolis: The Search Institute, 2010.

Biegel, G. "Mindfulness-Based Stress Reduction for Teens," 2019, https://www.stressedteens.com/training-for-professionals.

Breslau, J., S. E. Gilman, B. D. Stein, T. Ruder, T. Gmelin, and E. Miller. "Sex Differences in Recent First-Onset Depression in an Epidemiological Sample of Adolescents," *Translational Psychiatry* 7 (May 30, 2017): e1139.

Bridges, William B. and Susan Bridges. *Managing Transitions: Making the Most of Change.* Philadelphia: Da Capo Press, 2016.

Centers for Disease Control and Prevention. (2017). "Quick Stats: Suicide Rates for Teens Aged 15–19 Years, by Sex—United States, 1975–2015." *MMWR Morb Mortal Weekly Rept 2017*, 66:816: http://dx.doi.org/10.15585/mmwr.mm6630a6.

CIGNA, Ipsos. *CIGNA US Loneliness Index: Survey of 20,000 Americans Examining Behaviors Driving Loneliness in the United States.* 2018. https://www.cigna.com/assets/docs/ newsroom/loneliness-survey-2018-full-report.pdf.

Damour, L. *Untangled: Guiding Teenage Girls Through the Seven Transitions Into Adulthood.* New York: Ballantine Books, 2017.

Damour, L. *Under Pressure: Confronting the Epidemic of Stress and Anxiety in Girls.* New York: Ballantine Books, 2019.

Debold E., L. M. Brown, S. Weseen, and G. K. Brookins. "Cultivating Hardiness Zones for Adolescent Girls: A Reconceptualization of Resilience in Relationships with Caring Adults." In *Beyond Appearance: A New Look at Adolescent Girls*, edited by N.G. Johnson, M. C. Roberts, and J. Worell, 181–204. Washington: American Psychological Association, 1999.

Divecha, D. "Our Teens Are More Stressed Than Ever: Why, and What Can You Do About It?" *Developmental Science*, (May 9, 2019). https://www.developmentalscience.com/blog/2019/5/7/our-teens-are-more-stressed-than-ever.

Dweck, C. *Mindset: The New Psychology of Success.* New York: Ballantine Books, 2007.

Dweck, C. "Carol Dweck Revisits the Growth Mindset." *Education Week*, September 22, 2015, 20–24.

First Things First. "Brain Development." Accessed March 27, 2019. https://www.firstthingsfirst.org/early-childhood-matters/brain-development/.

Garringer, M. K. *Elements of Effective Practice for Mentoring, 4th Edition.* Boston: MENTOR: The National Mentoring Partnership, 2015.

Global EQ Community. "How to Practice Emotional Intelligence." Accessed November 25, 2018. https://www.6seconds.org/2018/03/28/emotional-intelligence-tips-choice/.

Godin, Seth. "You've arrived." *Seth's Blog*, July 30, 2017.

Goleman, D. and R. E. Boyatzis. "Emotional Intelligence Has 12 Elements. Which Do You Need to Work On?" *Harvard Business Review*, February 6, 2017.

Herrmann, N. and A. Herrmann-Nehdi. *The Whole Brain Business Book, Second Edition.* New York: McGraw-Hill, 2015.

Hinkelman, Lisa. *Girls Without Limits*. Thousand Oaks: Corwin, 2013.

Hinkelman, Lisa. *The Girls' Index: New Insights into the Complex World of Today's Girls*. Columbus: ROX Ruling Our Experiences, 2017.

Hopper, E. "The Study of Authenticity." HealthyPsych, February 12, 2018. https://healthypsych.com/the-study-of-authenticity/.

Impett, E. A. "Girls' Relationship Authenticity and Self-Esteem Across Adolescence." *Developmental Psychology*, (2008): 722–733.

Jensen, F. E. *The Teenage Brain*. New York: Harper Collins, 2015.

Johansen, B. *Get There Early: Sensing the Future to Compete in the Present*. San Francisco: Berrett-Koehler, 2007.

Johansen, B. *Leaders Make the Future*. San Francisco: Berrett-Koehler, 2012.

Johansen, B. *The New Leadership Literacies*. Oakland: Berrett-Koehler, 2017.

Khidekel, Marina. "10 Mindfulness Habits That Will Make You More Successful at Work." *Thrive Global*, March 15, 2019. https://thriveglobal.com/stories/mindfulness-tips-habits-success-focus-work/.

Marsh, Stephanie. "Teenagers on Loneliness: 'We Want to Talk to Our Parents. We Need Their Guidance.'" *Guardian*, April 8, 2017. https://www.theguardian.com/society/2017/apr/08/teenagers-loneliness-social-media-isolation-parents-attention.

Mitchinson, A. and R. Morris. *Learning About Learning Agility.* Greensboro: Center for Creative Leadership, 2014.

Murphey, D., T. Bandy, H. Schmitz, and K. Moore. "Research Brief – Caring Adults: Important for Positive Child Well-Being." Child Trends, 2013. https://www.childtrends.org/wp-content/uploads/2013/12/2013-54CaringAdults.pdf.

National Scientific Council on the Developing Child. "Supportive Relationships and Active Skill-Building Strengthen the Foundations of Resilience: Working Paper 13," 2015. https://developingchild.harvard.edu/resources/supportive-relationships-and-active-skill-building-strengthen-the-foundations-of-resilience/.

Niemiec, R. M. *The Power of Character Strengths.* Cincinnati: VIA Institute on Character, 2019.

Niemiec, R. M. "VIA Character Strengths: Research and Practice (The First 10 Years)." In *Well-being and Cultures: Perspectives on Positive Psychology*, edited by H. H. Knoop and A. Delle Fave, 11–30. New York: Springer, 2013.

Palmer, Parker J. "Circle of Trust Touchstones for Safe and Trustworthy Space." Adapted with permission from the Center for Courage and Renewal. Accessed April 10, 2019. http://www.couragerenewal.org/touchstones/.

Pipher, M. and S. Pipher Gilliam. *Reviving Ophelia: Saving the Selves of Adolescent Girls, Revised and Updated*. New York: Riverhead Books, 2019.

Price, V. C. *The Power of People: Four Kinds of People Who Can Change Your Life, 3rd Edition*. Minneapolis: JCAMA Publishers, 2006.

Rhodes, J. and E. Raposa. "Mentoring by the Numbers: Some Surprising Trends in Volunteer Efforts." *Chronicle of Evidence-Based Mentoring*, (July 2017).

Rock, D. *Handbook of NeuroLeadership*. London: NeuroLeadership Institute, 2013.

Roehlkepartain, E. C., K. Pekel, A. K. Syvertsen, J. Sethi, T. K. Sullivan, and P. C. Scales. *Relationships First: Creating Connections that Help Young People Thrive*. Minneapolis: Search Institute, 2017.

Sax, Leonard. *Girls on the Edge: The Four Factors Driving the New Crisis for Girls*. New York: Basic Books, 2010.

Scouller, J. *The Three Levels of Leadership*. Oxford: Management Books, 2016.

Senge, P. M. *Schools That Learn: A Fifth Discipline Fieldbook for Educators, Parents and Everyone Who Cares About Education*. New York: Crown Business, 2012.

Senge, P. M. *The Dawn of System Leadership.* Stanford: Leland Stanford Jr. University, 2015.

Shatkin, J. P. *Born to Be Wild: Why Teens Take Risks, and How We Can Keep Them Safe.* New York: Penguin Random House LLC, 2017.

Siegel, D. J. *Mindsight: The New Science of Personal Transformation.* New York: Bantom Books, 2011.

Siegel, D. J. and T. P. Bryson. *The Whole Brain Child: 12 Revolutionary Strategies to Nurture Your Child's Developing Mind.* New York: Bantam Books, 2012.

Siegel, D. J. *Brainstorm: The Power and Purpose of the Teenage Brain.* New York: The Penguin Group, 2013.

Siegel, D. J. *Mind: A Journey to the Heart of Being Human.* New York: W. W. Norton & Company, Inc., 2017.

Siegel, D. J. and T. P. Bryson. *The Power of Showing Up: How Parental Presence Shapes Who Our Kids Become and How Their Brains Get Wired.* New York: Ballantine Books, 2020.

Simmons, R. *Enough As She Is: How to Help Girls Move Beyond Impossible Standards of Success to Live Healthy, Happy, and Fulfilling Lives.* New York: Harper Collins, 2018.

Steinberg, Laurence. *Age of Opportunity: Lessons from the New Science of Adolescence.* New York: Houghton Mifflin Harcourt, 2014.

Steinem, G. *The Truth Will Set You Free, But First It Will Piss You Off!* New York: Random House, 2019.

Twenge, J. *iGen: Why Today's Super-Connected Kids Are Growing Up Less Rebellious, More Tolerant, Less Happy and Completely Unprepared for Adulthood.* New York: Atria Books, 2017.

Vo, D. X. *The Mindful Teen: Powerful Skills to Help You Handle Stress One Moment at a Time.* Oakland: New Harbinger Instant Help Books, 2015.

THE POWER OF
Natural Mentoring™

Experience
#ThePowerofNaturalMentoring

After reading this book, are you excited to contribute what you've learned from your life experiences to upcoming generations? Join Christine and a growing community of like-minded people to truly thrive in your Natural Mentoring relationships.

Complete **POWER2THRIVE**, a virtual course that actively explores the five components of the **THRIVE CYCLE** from the adolescent or professional Natural Mentoring perspective, visit the website, and sign up for email updates and information on live events and retreats.

Limited opportunities are also available for personal one-on-one coaching and organizational Natural Mentoring facilitation for your staff's professional development.

Contact the team at *Christine@ThePowerofNaturalMentoring.com* **to customize the right approach for you.**

Say hello and help us grow!
Share your Natural Mentoring experiences.
Use *#ThePowerofNaturalMentoring* **on**
any of the following social platforms:

- **Natural Mentoring**
- **ThePowerofNaturalMentoring**
- **CWagnerTweets**

ThePowerofNaturalMentoring.com